The Political
Consequences
of Being a Woman

Robert Y. Shapiro, Editor

Power, Conflict, and Democracy:
American Politics Into the Twenty-First Century

✺

This series focuses on how the will of the people and the public interest are promoted, encouraged, or thwarted. It aims to question not only the direction American politics will take as it enters the twenty-first century but also the direction American politics has already taken.

The series addresses the role of interest groups and social and political movements; openness in American politics; important developments in institutions such as the executive, legislative, and judicial branches at all levels of government as well as the bureaucracies thus created; the changing behavior of politicians and political parties; the role of public opinion; and the functioning of mass media. Because problems drive politics, the series also examines important policy issues in both domestic and foreign affairs.

The series welcomes all theoretical perspectives, methodologies, and types of evidence that answer important questions about trends in American politics.

The Political Consequences of Being a Woman

How Stereotypes Influence the Conduct and Consequences of Political Campaigns

Kim Fridkin Kahn

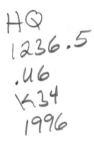

Columbia University Press
New York

Columbia University Press
New York   Chichester, West Sussex

Copyright © 1996 Columbia University Press
All rights reserved

Library of Congress Cataloging-in-Publication Data
Kahn, Kim Fridkin.
  The political consequences of being a woman : how stereotypes
influence the conduct and consequences of political campaigns / Kim
Fridkin Kahn.
    p. cm. — (Power, conflict, and democracy)
  Includes bibliographical references and index.
  ISBN 0–231–10302–6 (cloth : alk. paper). — ISBN 0–231–10303–4
  (pbk. : alk. paper)
    1. Women in politics—United States. 2. Electioneering—United
States. 3. Mass media—Political aspects—United States. 4. Press
and politics—United States. 5. Stereotype (Psychology)—United
States.   I. Title.   II. Series.
HQ1236.5.U6K34   1996
306.2'083—dc20   96–10979

⊗

Casebound editions of Columbia University Press books are printed on
permanent and durable acid-free paper.

Printed in the United States of America

c 10 9 8 7 6 5 4 3 2 1
p 10 9 8 7 6 5 4 3 2 1

For Jim and Jennifer

Contents

Acknowledgments

This book began when I was at the University of Michigan. At Michigan, Philip E. Converse, Michael W. Traugott, Hazel Markus, and especially Edie N. Goldenberg provided me with much guidance, encouragement, and insightful advice. At Arizona State University, the project evolved a great deal. My colleagues, Rick Herrera and Warren E. Miller, read early versions of chapters and offered me careful and helpful suggestions. I am especially indebted to Patrick Kenney who read and provided feedback on several versions of this manuscript and whose support and constructive criticism helped me a great deal. For reading through early versions of the book, I would like to thank Donald R. Kinder, Virginia Sapiro and Donna Wasserman. Their thoughtful reactions helped me rework and improve the book.

I am also indebted to a number of research assistants for their assistance with the coding of the newspapers and the running of the experiments: Jennifer Crookes, Amy Cuzzola, Paula Drury, Abby Dupke, Barbara Fridkin, Roberta Gibbons, Patti Webb, and especially Virginia Chanley. Julian Kanter at the University of Oklahoma Political Commercial Archive provided me with access to the political commercials of the senate and gubernatorial candidates. I also want to thank Pat Crittenden for her editorial suggestions.

While at Michigan, several grants from the Rackham Graduate School as well as a fellowship from the Earhart Foundation helped me with initial data collection activities. At Arizona State University, the CLAS Mini-grant, the Faculty Grant-In-Aid, and the Women's Studies Summer Research Award helped me continue to collect data as well as write initial chapters of the book.

Early versions of some of the chapters are reprinted with permission as follows:

"Gender Differences in Campaign Messages: The Political Advertisements of Men and Women Candidates for U.S. Senate" in the *Political Research Quarterly* 46, no. 3 (September 1993): 481–502 (by permission of the University of Utah, Copyright Holder);

"Women Candidates in the News: An Examination of Gender Differences in U.S. Senate Campaigns" (with Edie N. Goldenberg) in *Public Opinion Quarterly* 55 (1991) (by permission of The Chicago University Press; © 1991 by The University of Chicago. All rights reserved);

"Does Being Male Help: An Investigation of the Effects of Candidates' Campaign Coverage on Evaluation of U.S. Senate Candidates" in the *Journal of Politics* 54, no. 2 (1992): 497–517 (by permission of the University of Texas Press);

"The Distorted Mirror: Press Coverage of Women Candidates for State-wide Office" in the *Journal of Politics* 56, no. 1 (1994): 154–73 (by permission of the University of Texas Press);

"Does Gender Make a Difference? An Experimental Examination of Sex Stereotypes and Press Patterns in Statewide Campaigns" in the *American Journal of Political Science* 38 (1994): 162–95 (by permission of The University of Wisconsin Press).

I would like to express my appreciation to my parents for their confidence and encouragement. Finally, and most important, I want to thank my husband and my daughter for their support, understanding, and love.

The Political Consequences of Being a Woman

1
Introduction

✸

In 1992 Patty Murray ran for the U.S. Senate seat in Washington as "a mom in tennis shoes." Murray's description of her candidacy encouraged voters to consider her gender when casting their vote. This strategy was immensely successful in a climate where political insiders were viewed with skepticism and issues such as health care reform topped the political agenda. While being a woman appeared to be an asset in 1992, it is often a liability. An article on the front page of the *New York Times* warned, "In 1994, 'Vote for Woman' Does Not Play So Well." During this election crime was a central issue in many races, and women candidates suffered because they were not viewed as tough enough on crime.

Women's changing fortunes in electoral politics are driven by the correspondence between people's stereotypical images of women candidates and the salient issues of the day. In this book I explain how women's perceived capabilities and liabilities influence the conduct and consequences of political campaigns. I theorize that people's stereotypical beliefs about male and female candidates influence the candidates' behavior, the news media's campaign coverage, and the views of voters. In addition, I show how the consequences of these stereotypes vary with the electoral climate—women candidates have an advantage in some settings and are at a disadvantage in others.

To begin, people's preconceptions about the strengths and weaknesses of women candidates influence how candidates present themselves to the electorate. For example, in adopting a campaign strategy, women candidates may choose to emphasize themes that are consistent with people's stereotypical views of them, because women candidates may view these themes as more effective.

Similarly, when covering candidates for statewide offices, reporters and editors are likely to consider their views about typical male and female candidates. Reliance on stereotypes could encourage reporters to ask women candidates different questions from those addressed to men, leading reporters to stress different issues when covering these candidates. If the news media treat men and women candidates differently, these differences can affect their political fortunes.

Finally, voters own stereotypical views of candidates can influence their choices between candidates. Reinforced by the candidate's behavior and presentations by the news media, these stereotypes are likely to influence voters' views of men and women candidates. In particular, if voters have different images of men and women candidates, these images will influence their views about the abilities of the candidates and, ultimately, their voting decisions.

Figure 1.1 illustrates the role that stereotypes are expected to play in electoral campaigns. People's stereotypical images of men and women will directly affect the behavior of candidates, the press's treatment of these candidates, and the voters' evaluations of them. In addition, stereotypical images of candidates will influence voters indirectly, since voters obtain their information about the electoral contest from the candidates and the media.

In addition, the consequences of these stereotypes will change with the electoral context. When the salient issues and traits of the campaign complement a woman candidate's stereotypical strengths, women will receive an advantage from stereotypes. In contrast, when the important campaign themes correspond to a woman's perceived weaknesses, people's stereotypes will hinder her in her bid for office. The correspondence between the campaign context and people's stereotypical images will determine whether women will be ultimately helped or hurt.

FIGURE 1.1   *The Impact of Sex Stereotypes in Political Campaigns*

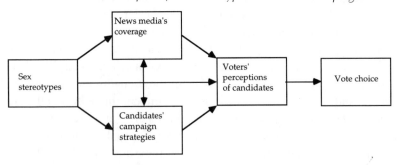

This book focuses exclusively on races for governor and senator. I chose these two offices because they are among the most influential in the United States and because by looking at them I can examine how the impact of stereotypes is affected by the electoral climate. In U.S. Senate races the salient issues in the campaign often correspond to a woman candidate's stereotypical weaknesses such as foreign policy, defense issues, and the economy. In contrast, the important issues in gubernatorial campaigns usually highlight a woman candidate's perceived strengths such as health and education. By showing how the electoral context conditions the effect of sex stereotypes, this book provides insights into the important characteristics and impact of women's political campaigns.

Because stereotypes are central to this book, the next section defines stereotypes and describes how they influence people's worldviews. I then illustrate the impact of stereotypes on voters' views of men and women candidates. The subsequent sections demonstrate how stereotypes affect the news media's coverage of campaigns as well as candidates' choices of campaign strategy, and they describe how stereotypes help women candidates in certain settings but hurt them in others.

The Nature of Stereotypes

Seventy years ago, in a seminal book on public opinion, Lippman (1922) argued that people use stereotypes because "modern life is hurried and multifarious [and] there is neither time nor opportunity for intimate acquaintance." Instead, when people observe others, they notice a trait (e.g., gender) that signifies membership in a particular group (e.g., women), and they complete the picture by means of the stereotypes they carry in their heads. (Lippman 1922:59). According to Lippman, by classifying an individual as a member of a particular group (e.g., a woman), people can draw inferences about the individual based on the individual's membership in the group (e.g., she is woman and therefore compassionate).

Over the years cognitive psychologists have substantiated Lippman's view that stereotypes simplify people's complex social environments (e.g., Bodenhausen and Wyer 1985; Fiske and Neuberg 1990; Tajfel 1969). Unlike early researchers who viewed stereotypes as pathological or evil (for a review see Ashmore and Del Boca 1981), researchers now consider stereotyping a normal cognitive process. People do not have the cognitive resources necessary to view every new person as unique, so they rely on stereotypes to simplify their perceptions.

A stereotype can be thought of as a cognitive structure that contains a set of expectations about a certain group or category (Fiske and Neuberg 1990; Hamilton 1979). People's well-organized ideas about the attributes and characteristics of social groups allow them to process new information more efficiently (Cantor and Mischel 1979; Fiske and Linville 1990; Taylor 1981). By relying on stored information about groups, people limit the amount of new information that they need to draw conclusions about an individual.

When developing impressions of others, people routinely give priority to judgments based on stereotypes rather than judgments based on new information (Fiske and Neuberg 1990). People prefer to limit their cognitive efforts by drawing stereotypical impressions rather than processing new information that may alter their initial impressions.

When people stereotype, they select social or physical characteristics to discriminate and manage information. Race and sex, among others, are likely to be used since they are easily identifiable and people have well-developed ideas about the attributes of these categories (Taylor, Fiske, Etcoff, and Ruderman 1978). People place others into such social groups and process information based on this categorization. By classifying an individual as a member of a social group, a person (or perceiver) gains insights into the characteristics of the individual (Fiske and Neuberg 1990). This makes certain types of information more accessible, which leads the perceiver to draw certain conclusions about the individual. For instance, after identifying a candidate as an African American, a voter may conclude that the candidate is a Democrat who favors affirmative action programs.

The act of stereotyping encourages the confirmation of preexisting stereotypes (Hamilton 1979). First, the process of categorization encourages people to attend to information that is consistent with their overall impressions. Second, the process encourages people to interpret new information as supportive of their initial categorization. Consequently, these processes bias memory in the direction of a consistency that maintains the status quo because it reinforces preexisting stereotypes.

Consider the following example: a voter labels a candidate as a liberal, which leads the voter to look for certain details about the candidate (e.g., the candidate's position on abortion, the candidate's commitment to protection of the environment). In addition, the voter may interpret any available information as confirming the voter's categorization of the candidate as a liberal. For instance, a voter may interpret the candidate's opposition to a budget deficit reduction package as illustrative of a tax-and-spend philosophy; however, the candidate's opposition to the package may stem from the belief that the plan does not call for enough budget cuts. Finally, after stereotyping the candidate as a liberal, the voter is likely to remember information consistent with this (e.g., the candidate's pro-environment stand), while forgetting less consistent information (e.g., the candidate's prolife position).

While impressions driven by stereotypes are always more efficient than those based on newly acquired information, certain factors may accentuate stereotyping. First, when confronted with a difficult cognitive task, an individual is likely to rely on stereotypes to draw conclusions. For example, if a voter is presented with a plethora of policy information about two relatively unknown candidates and is asked to choose between the candidates, the voter may turn to partisan schemas or stereotypes to help process the political information (Rahn 1993). The reliance on party as a stereotype helps the voter choose between the competing candidates.

In addition, stereotyping will be more common when a person needs to draw conclusions about an individual but lacks the relevant data to do so (Riggle, Ottati, Wyer, Kuklinski, and Schwarz 1992). For instance, a citizen goes to the polls to vote for president and is confronted with a list of unknown candidates for lower level offices. The only information available to the voter is each candidate's name and party affiliation. In such a situation the voter may rely on the candidates' party as a cue, because the voter assumes that Democrats and Republicans will differ in predictable ways.

The salience of such a category will also promote greater stereotyping (Higgins, Rholes, and Jones 1977; Wyer and Srull 1980). If an individual has recently used a category such as party to process information, then it will be more accessible and will more likely be used when forming impressions. During campaigns candidates try to make certain characteristics salient as a way of "priming" voters to consider specific criteria when judging candidates (Iyengar and Kinder 1987; Jacobs and Shapiro 1994). For instance, in the 1990 U.S. Senate race in North Carolina, Jesse Helms may have decided to stress affirmative action in his campaign as a way of activating people's schemas about race. If Helms was successful, then North Carolina voters were likely to consider their stereotypes about African Americans when choosing between Jesse Helms and Harvey Gantt, the first African American to win a major statewide nomination in North Carolina.

In addition, factors that make an individual's characteristics especially salient will elicit greater stereotyping (Taylor 1981). For instance, in a group composed of a single woman and several men, gender will be prominent.

People observing the group are likely to draw stereotypical impressions of the female member. In the U.S. Senate there are only 8 women out of 100 senators, and observers watching the deliberations of most committees will view one woman working with a large number of men. Such a configuration is likely to make the gender of the female member salient, thereby encouraging stereotyping the woman senator.

Finally, an individual's motivation, time, and resources are related to the degree of stereotyping (Pratto and Bargh 1991). If someone has only a limited time to draw a conclusion about an individual, and if that person is not particularly motivated to make an accurate impression, then he or she is likely to rely on stereotypes. On the other hand, if the goal is to draw a faithful representation of the individual, then the person may ignore his or her global impressions and collect information directly from the individual.

Substance of Sex Stereotypes

In addition to establishing the nature of stereotypes, psychologists have demonstrated the pervasiveness of stereotypes in general and of sex stereotypes in particular (Ashmore, Del Boca, and Wohlers 1986; Broverman, Vogel, Broverman, Clarkson, and Rosenkrantz 1972; Deaux and Lewis 1984; Williams and Best 1990). Sex stereotypes are defined as a cognitive structure of inferential relations that link personal attributes, behaviors, and beliefs to the social categories of male and female (Ashmore and Del Boca 1979; Deaux and Lewis 1984). When a person categorizes another on the basis of the individual's gender, he or she infers the existence of gender-related characteristics consistent with the initial categorization.

Sex stereotypes lead people to view women as possessing expressive strengths — that they are emotional, understanding, gentle, warm, compassionate, while men are viewed as possessing instrumental strengths — they are independent, objective, ambitious, aggressive, knowledgeable (Ashmore and Del Boca 1979; Broverman et al. 1972; Deaux and Lewis 1984; Ruble 1983). People's conceptions of the typical man and woman do not appear to be a result of education, socioeconomic status, or religion (Broverman et al. 1972). In addition, sex stereotypes are not a uniquely American phenomenon. On the contrary, William and Best's (1990) recent work documents sex stereotypes in each of the ten countries studied: Australia, Brazil, France, Germany, Italy, Norway, Nigeria, Pakistan, Peru, and the United States. Finally, a number of studies find that men and women hold similar views regarding typically male and female characteristics (Ashmore, Del Boca, and Wohlers 1986; Broverman et al. 1972; Ruble 1983; Williams and Best 1990).

Stereotypical views of men and women influence how people think and behave. Deaux and Enswiller (1974) found that subjects attribute skill to a man's successful performance at a masculine task, while the same performance by a woman is attributed to luck. Similarly, Feather and Simon (1975) show that people will assign personal credit to a man's success, while they will assign blame for a woman's failure.

Deaux (1984) theorizes that these gender differences in causal attribution are driven by commonly held stereotypes about men and women. Men are expected to do better than women—especially at masculine tasks—and when they fulfill expectations, their success is attributed to skill. When men fail, their failure is attributed to bad luck. Women, on the other hand, are expected to do poorly—especially at masculine tasks. When women fail and thereby confirm expectations, their failure is attributed to their lack of ability; when they succeed, their success is attributed to luck.

In addition, researchers have shown that stereotypes can influence the behavior of stereotyped individuals: a stereotyped person may modify his or her behavior based on the observers' stereotypical perceptions (Hamilton 1979; Zanna and Pack 1975). In a study of impression formation, Zanna and Pack (1975) examined the behavior of undergraduate women who expected to interact with men who held either traditional or nontraditional views of women. When told that their male partners were desirable potential dates, the women portrayed themselves as traditional or nontraditional, depending on the men's views. These results suggest that stereotypes are self-perpetuating; they elicit stereotypical behavior from people who have been stereotyped by others.

Sex Stereotypes in the Political Arena

Scholars interested in explaining the paucity of women in elective office have examined the impact of sex stereotypes in political campaigns. Some researchers have examined sex stereotypes indirectly by looking at whether women candidates receive less support than men at the polls. Using both aggregate election statistics and survey data, these studies fail to show that women consistently receive fewer votes than their male counterparts (Darcy, Welch, and Clark 1987; Darcy and Schramm 1977; Welch, Ambrosious, Clark, and Darcy 1985; Zipp and Plutzer 1985). However, this line of research is not well suited for assessing sex stereotypes, since it is difficult to isolate the impact of gender on vote choice. In particular, many factors are related to the gender of the candidate (e.g., qualifications, background, incumbency, party, and political climate), making it difficult to conclude that women receive less support simply because they are women.

Given the limitation of this research, scholars have used alternative methods to measure the impact of sex stereotypes more directly. Survey researchers have asked respondents whether they are just as likely to vote for a "qualified woman" as a "qualified man" for a particular office. This research shows that people are less supportive of women candidates and that their support declines with the increasing prestige of the office (Darcy, Welch, and Clark 1987; Gallup 1984; National Women's Political Caucus (NWPC) 1987; Sigelman and Welch 1984; Wells and Smeal 1974).

Complementing the psychological research on sex stereotypes, surveys fail to find differences in men's and women's support for women candidates (Gallup 1984; NWPC 1987; Welch and Sigelman 1982).

While demonstrating clear differences in support for qualified men and women candidates, some studies may be flawed by social desirability demands. That is, the wording of the survey questions may make it undesirable to "vote" against a woman candidate simply because of her gender. For example, in the Hedlund, Freeman, Hamm, and Stein (1979) study, the researchers asked respondents, "If two candidates for school board are equally qualified except one is a woman and the other is a man, for whom would you vote?" In such a situation, respondents are asked to indicate whether they would choose between two candidates based solely on gender. Given that respondents are likely to understand the purpose of such studies—to uncover voter sexism—they may respond in a socially desirable fashion, thus concealing their authentic attitudes toward women in politics. The surveys' potential social desirability problems may have led scholars to underestimate the effect of gender on voting.

In addition to examining support for "qualified" candidates, surveys have explored gender differences in trait evaluations for "typical" male and female candidates. These studies parallel the psychological research on sex stereotyping by showing that male candidates are viewed as stable, aggressive, decisive, tough, and competent, while women are viewed as trustworthy, compassionate, honest, and moral (Boles and Durio 1980; Boles and Durio 1981; NWPC 1987).

These surveys also illustrate that male or female candidates are viewed as better able to deal with particular issues. As Huddy and Terkildsen (1993) explain, stereotypes regarding women's compassionate nature and men's competence and aggressiveness encourage people to view men and women as having alternative areas of expertise. Specifically, male candidates are considered better able to deal with foreign policy, the economy, defense spending, arms control, foreign trade, and farm issues; female candidates are considered better able to deal with day care, poverty, education, health care, civil rights, drug abuse, and the environment (Gallup 1984, NWPC 1987).

Finally, experimental methods have been used to examine sex stereotyping by voters. A prototype for much of the subsequent experimental work, Sapiro (1981–1982) examined subjects' evaluations of male and female candidates by giving subjects a speech by Senator Howard Baker that had no clear ideological or party leanings. She told some subjects that John Leeds, a candidate for the House, had given the speech, while other subjects thought that the speech was made by house candidate Joan Leeds. With this design, Sapiro could see whether the candidate's gender influenced people's evaluations of equivalent male and female candidates.

The research by Sapiro and others demonstrates that people develop distinct impressions of men and women candidates (Adams 1975; Ekstrand and Eckert 1981; Huddy and Terkildsen 1993; Leeper 1991; Mend, Bell, and Bath 1976; Rosenwasser and Seale 1988; Rosenwasser, Rogers, Fling, Silver-Pickens, and Butemeyer 1987; Sapiro 1981–1982; Sigelman and Sigelman 1984; Spohn and Gillespie 1987). Women candidates are viewed as more compassionate and honest, while men are considered more knowledgeable and stronger leaders. In addition, women are viewed as more competent in certain policy areas (education, health, environment, maintaining honesty and integrity in government, helping the disabled and aged) while the expertise of male candidates resides in alternative domains (e.g., military, farm policy, foreign policy, the economy).

Unlike survey studies that fail to find differences in men's and women's support for female candidates, some experimental studies find that women subjects are more likely than male subjects to support female candidates (Mend, Bell, and Bath 1976; Sigelman and Sigelman 1982; and Spohn and Gillespie 1987). This disparity between surveys and experiments may be due to differences in sampling strategies. Specifically, national random samples of adults (eighteen years and older) are interviewed in the survey studies, while college and high school students are recruited as subjects in the experiments. It may be that young women in the experiments are more supportive of women candidates, while adult men and women are equally supportive of women candidates.

While these studies demonstrate the impact of sex stereotypes on people's impressions of male and female candidates, they have limitations. First, all of the experimental studies rely on students as subjects, thereby reducing the generalizability of their results. Since students, who are the youngest voters, may have the most favorable attitudes toward women candidates, experiments using a more representative sample may yield different patterns of sex stereotyping.

Second, in many of the experiments, subjects are provided with very little information about the candidate, besides the candidate's gender. In the study by Rosenwasser et al. (1987), for instance, subjects were given a three-sentence paragraph describing the candidate. In this low information environment, the candidate's gender will be especially salient to subjects, thereby promoting more stereotyping. An experiment that replicates the electoral setting more realistically by providing more information to potential voters may produce lower levels of sex stereotyping.

In summary, studies examining sex stereotypes among voters show that people consider the candidate's gender when forming impressions. Using different designs and exploring different aspects of candidate evaluation, these studies demonstrate that people hold and use sex stereotypes to draw distinctions between male and female candidates.

The Campaign Strategies of the Candidates

Candidates of both sexes may consciously consider people's stereotypical images of their candidacies when adopting strategies for their electoral campaigns. Acknowledging common views about the typical capabilities and liabilities of male and female candidates, candidates are likely to believe that certain campaign appeals will be more effective than others. For example, since women are viewed as less assertive than men, women are expected to be less verbally aggressive in their electoral campaigns (Trent and Friedenberg 1983). If women candidates flout these expectations by initiating aggressive and forceful attacks, they may be viewed more negatively by voters. Therefore women may be more likely than men to refrain from "attack" advertising.

Similarly, people's stereotypes about candidates can influence the types of issues on which candidates choose to concentrate in their campaign appeals. Since voters' issue priorities are responsive to the media's emphasis, candidates try to influence these priorities by emphasizing their stereotypical strengths during their campaigns. Given this strategy, women may choose to concentrate on such issues as education and health policy, while men may stress their commitment to such issues as the economy and defense policy. By stressing these alternative domains, male and female candidates will "prime" issues that will uniquely benefit their own candidacies. For example, by spending a great deal of time discussing educational issues, a woman candidate hopes to lead voters to believe that education is an important issue. Thus voters may begin to think about educational issues when evaluating the candidate and her opponent. By influencing the candidate's choice of campaign strategies, stereotypes can directly influence the candidate's behavior and may indirectly influence the media's coverage and voters' reactions to the campaign.

Of course, a candidate's choice of campaign strategy may be less calculated. Just as Zanna and Pack (1975) found that undergraduate women unconsciously modified their behavior in response to the stereotypical views of their potential dates, women candidates may inadvertently present themselves in ways consistent with voters' stereotypical beliefs. As a way of gaining approval, women candidates may unintentionally reinforce stereotypes by choosing to emphasize personality traits and policy priorities that are consistent with voters' stereotypical views of women.

The strategies that candidates choose to implement are consequential since candidates can influence the impressions of voters both directly and indirectly. First, effective campaigners can influence the news media's coverage of the campaign by framing the contest in ways favorable to their candidacies (e.g., Jacobs and Shapiro 1994; Popkin 1991). In addition, candidates can influence voters directly via such controlled communications as political commercials. By presenting new information (e.g., Patterson and McClure 1976) and by emphasizing certain considerations (e.g., Garramone, Steele, and Pinkleton 1991; Schleuder, McCombs, and Wanta 1991), political commercials can affect citizens' views of male and female candidates.

The News Media's Role in Campaigns

Newspeople, like candidates, are likely to consider commonly held stereotypes when covering men and women candidates for statewide office. Reliance on these stereotypes, which cut across education and income levels, are likely to create differences in the amount and substance of coverage given to male and female candidates. If the press distinguish between male and female candidates in their coverage, these differences will affect voters' views of the candidates, thereby influencing the electability of women candidates.

The media's impact on the political arena has received a great deal of study. Although early studies suggested that the media largely reinforced people's predispositions (for a review of the "minimal effects" literature, see Klapper 1960), recent work documents more substantial media effects. Ansolabehere, Behr, and Iyengar (1991) identify four distinct media effects in electoral campaigns: information acquisition, persuasion, agenda-setting, and priming.

First, the news media influence both the amount and type of information that voters acquire during campaigns. For instance, both Aldrich (1980) and Patterson (1980) find a strong relationship between news coverage of the 1976 presidential campaign and public awareness of Jimmy Carter. In addition, the media's emphasis on campaign issues such as the horse race and gaffes rather than on policy issues influences the public's view of electoral campaigns. Research at the presidential level shows that most people think about the game rather than the substance of the campaign and about campaign issues rather than policy issues (Brady and Johnston 1987; Joslyn 1984; Patterson 1980). Furthermore, Patterson's (1980) study of the 1976 presidential campaign shows that the media influence people's assessments of a candidate's viability. Since viability and electability evaluations can influence vote choice (Bartels 1988; Brady and Johnston 1987), the news media's emphasis on the horse race has important electoral implications.

In addition to relaying information to potential voters, exposure to the media can change people's attitudes toward both political candidates and events. Both experimental and quasi-experimental studies (e.g. Paletz and Vinegar 1977; Robinson 1976; Steeper 1978), as well as aggregate time-series analyses (MacKuen 1983; Page and Shapiro 1987), suggest that the news media can produce changes in public opinion.

Agenda-setting, a third type of media effect, has been studied most extensively by media scholars. The theory of agenda-setting suggests that by focusing on certain issues and ignoring others, the news media decide which issues people will consider most important (e.g., Erbring, Goldenberg, and Miller 1980; Iyengar and Kinder 1987; Iyengar, Peters, and Kinder 1982; MacKuen 1981; Weaver, Graber, McCombs, Eyal 1981). Although most researchers have uncovered some evidence for agenda-setting, the strength of the phenomenon varies considerably for different issues and individuals. For example, agenda-setting is more powerful for "faraway" issues, such as Vietnam and campus unrest (e.g., Mackuen 1981; Weaver et al. 1981). Similarly, certain individuals are more susceptible to agenda-setting. In particular, people especially sensitive to an issue, those dependent on the news media for information, and those with lower levels of political interest are more likely to be influenced by changes in the news media's agenda (Erbring, Goldenberg, and Miller 1980; Iyengar and Kinder 1987; Iyengar, Peters, and Kinder 1982; Weaver et al. 1981).

The priming phenomenon, an offshoot of agenda-setting, suggests that by emphasizing certain issues, the news media alter the criteria people use to evaluate public officials (e.g., Iyengar and Kinder 1987; Iyengar, Peters, and Kinder 1982). For example, if the news media concentrate their coverage on economic issues, the public will come to think that economic issues are important (agenda-setting). Consequently, voters' evaluations of the president's performance on economic issues will strongly influence their overall evaluations of the president. The priming phenomenon has been documented both experimentally (Iyengar and Kinder 1987; Iyengar, Peters, and Kinder 1982) and with survey data (Krosnick and Kinder 1990). Priming is a potentially powerful phenomenon, suggesting that the news media can influence people's views of political candidates by influencing what people think about when evaluating competing candidates.

Given citizens' reliance on the news media for information, and given the news media's potential impact on people's perceptions of politics, gender differences in news coverage of political candidates can be consequential. If, like the public at large, reporters and editors hold stereotypical views of men and women, then these stereotypes may influence coverage patterns. By differentiating between male and female candidates in their coverage, the press may encourage voters to develop more favorable impressions of certain candidates and less favorable images of others. The media's representation of a candidate's campaign may therefore influence the electability of candidates.

The scarcity of women senators and governors makes the female candidate's gender especially salient to journalists, thereby encouraging greater stereotyping. These stereotypes may influence the way in which male and female candidacies are presented in the news. For example, newspeople could hold certain preconceptions about women candidates that lead them to consider those candidates less viable than their male counterparts. If this is the case, then women are likely to receive less news coverage than comparable male candidates. This potential difference in the quantity of coverage can influence the electability of the candidates, because these candidates will be less widely known and voters may be less willing to support their candidacies.

In addition to gender differences in the amount of coverage, stereotypical views are likely to influence the substance of news coverage. As a way of cutting cognitive costs, reporters may give priority to gender-based stereotypes when covering candidates. If this is the case, reporters may emphasize a woman candidate's compassion, while stressing a male candidate's leadership ability. This hypothesized difference in patterns of coverage, driven by gender-based stereotypes, is potentially powerful, since the news media can influence what voters consider when evaluating candidates. Hence voters may consider a woman candidate's compassion and a male candidate's leadership qualities when evaluating candidates for office.

Gender differences in news coverage are unlikely to be equally consequential in all electoral contests. Instead, because the influence of the news media grows with the size of the constituency (Goldenberg and Traugott 1984; Goldenberg and Traugott 1987), gender differences in news coverage are potentially more consequential in national and statewide elections than in local contests. Races for the House of Representatives generate very little news coverage and incumbents dominate the small amount of coverage that does exist (Clarke and Evans 1983; Goldenberg and Traugott 1984), so that gender differences in news attention are likely to be less important. However, in statewide races for the U.S. Senate and governor where media coverage is more prevalent, gender differences in news attention could be more influential.

The Context of the Campaign

People rely on sex stereotypes to distinguish between male and female candidates, and these stereotypical views reinforce the idea that women possess certain traits (e.g., compassion, honesty) while men possess other traits (e.g., leadership, competence). Given these stereotypes, certain campaign settings provide more opportunities for women candidates, just as other settings offer more obstacles. In particular, when characteristics of the electoral climate place a premium on women's stereotypical strengths, women will have an advantage. In contrast, when the campaign setting emphasizes women's perceived weaknesses, women will be at a disadvantage.

In races for statewide office, campaigns for governor offer women a more favorable campaign climate than do races for senator. The relevant issue domains in gubernatorial races are more likely to correspond to women's stereotypical strengths, while the salient issues in senate races tend to correspond to their perceived weaknesses. Because of the senate's constitutional policy responsibilities, foreign policy and national security issues are more important in U.S. Senate races (Sabato 1983; Stein 1990). In gubernatorial races, on the other hand, statewide issues such as education and health care are more relevant (Sabato 1983; Seroka 1980; Tidmarch, Hyman, and Sorkin 1984).

The news media coverage of gubernatorial and senate campaigns documents the distinctive agendas of these two offices (Kahn 1995). In a content analysis of the largest circulating newspaper in twenty-six senate races and twenty-four gubernatorial races in the 1980s, Kahn found that almost one-third (29%) of all issue coverage in senate races focused on foreign policy and defense, while less than one percent of the coverage in gubernatorial campaigns mentioned such issues. In gubernatorial races, social programs and social issues received almost twice as much coverage as they do in senate races (57% v. 33%).

Since these alternative issue domains parallel the stereotypical strengths of male and female candidates, women may have an easier time running for governor than for senator. In campaigns for both offices, women candidates are likely to emphasize issues that correspond to their traditional strengths. Yet these issue priorities will probably receive press attention in gubernatorial races. If this is the case, women candidates for governor will have an easier time influencing the news media's agenda and thereby influencing the priorities of voters. In races for governor, voters will consider issues such as education and health reform when they evaluate competing candidates. Given common stereotypes and the salient issues in gubernatorial races, people are likely to develop more favorable views of women candidates.

In U.S. Senate races, on the other hand, women candidates may emphasize the same issues as their gubernatorial counterparts. However, their campaign messages is likely to be ignored, since the press consider economic issues and foreign policy to be more relevant in senate races. Given this scenario, voters will be encouraged to think about economic and foreign policy issues when comparing male and female senate candidates, which could lead voters to develop more positive impressions of male candidates.

This book examines the ways in which people's stereotypical images of men and women candidates shape campaigns for statewide office. By looking at the campaign process, I examine how stereotypes influence the actions of candidates, the news media, and voters. I chose senate and gubernatorial campaigns to illustrate how the consequences of sex stereotypes vary with the electoral setting. To examine the multiple actors in the campaign, I collected three distinct sources of evidence based on two complementary research approaches.

Chapter 2 describes the research strategy of the study and illustrates the advantages of my multimethod approach.

I begin by examining the impact of stereotypes in U.S. Senate elections where women's perceived weaknesses are highlighted. Chapter 3 looks systematically at differences in the way men and women campaign for the senate. By looking at the style and substance of the candidates' advertisements, I show how expectations about the capabilities and liabilities of men and women influence the choice of campaign strategies. In addition, I compare the candidates' political advertisements with news coverage of these campaigns to see how responsive the news media are to men and women's campaigns.

In chapter 4 I look more extensively at how men and women are treated by the news media in Senate races. The results of content analysis of news reports show that female candidates do not receive the same press treatment as men. Women receive less news coverage, and the coverage they do receive focuses more on their viability and less on their positions on policy issues. Furthermore, the press's discussion of the candidate's viability is more negative for women candidates than for men.

Chapter 5 explores the impact of differences in news coverage on people's impressions of men and women senate candidates. I use an experimental study to recreate the gender differences noted in the content analysis of news coverage. With this experiment, I also look at whether voters think about the candidates' sex when forming impressions and whether gender differences in coverage and voters' sex stereotypes cumulatively influence voters' views of senate candidates.

In chapter 6 I turn to how changes in the context of the campaign influence the electoral fortunes of women candidates by looking at elections for governor. In contrast to senate campaigns where the prominent issues in the campaign tend to correspond to women's perceived weaknesses, the important campaign themes in gubernatorial elections often complement women's stereotypical strengths. In this chapter I look at how changes in the prevailing electoral setting influence how candidates campaign for office. In particular, I examine the political commercials of candidates running for governor between 1982 and 1988 and compare these messages to those presented by senate candidates.

Chapter 7 looks at patterns of news coverage in gubernatorial campaigns to see whether the press distinguish between male and female gubernatorial candidates in their campaign coverage. This analysis demonstrates that the press differentiates between male and female candidates in their coverage, although the differences are less dramatic for gubernatorial candidates than for senate candidates. Coverage of female gubernatorial candidates, for example, is more likely to focus on the candidates' personality characteristics than on the candidates' issue concerns.

In chapter 8 I rely on the experimental design developed in earlier chapters to examine the effect of news media's coverage and sex stereotypes on people's views of male and female candidates for governor. The results of these experiments demonstrate that, compared to senate races, gender differences in press treatment are more equitable and do not lead to impressive differences in evaluations of male and female gubernatorial candidates. In addition, people's reliance on sex stereotypes produces more positive evaluations of women gubernatorial candidates, compared to their male colleagues.

Chapter 9 examines the electoral significance of stereotypes. Relying on survey data, I look at how the context of the campaign influences the electability of women candidates running for the U.S. Senate between 1988 and 1992. The results of this analysis indicate that women candidates are viewed more favorably and receive more votes when they run in a campaign highlighting their stereotypical strengths. Drawing the book's studies together, the final chapter offers conclusions about how people's reliance on stereotypes influences the campaign process in profound ways. Notions about "typical" male and female candidates create significant obstacles for women in certain electoral environments, while these notions produce distinct advantages for women in other settings. In addition, the pervasiveness of such stereotypes affects the quality of political representation in the United States.

2

Stereotypes in Statewide Campaigns

☼

Do common conceptions about the capabilities and liabilities of women candidates influence the behavior of the news media, the candidates, and voters? Given the comprehensive nature of this inquiry, I use a multimethod design to answer this question. In addition, I examine the role of stereotypes in senate and gubernatorial campaigns to see whether the impact of stereotypes varies with the electoral climate.

I begin by looking at whether candidates consider common beliefs about men and women when developing their campaign tactics. To examine the choice of strategies, I analyze the content of candidates' televised political advertisements. Since candidates may stress their stereotypical strengths in races where these strengths are highlighted, while downplaying these traits in other settings, I examine campaign appeals in both senate and gubernatorial campaigns.

If men and women pursue strategies consistent with their stereotypical strengths, then news coverage of their campaigns is likely to reflect this emphasis. However, even if men and women disregard stereotypical images of their candidacies when campaigning, the news media may, nevertheless, cover their campaigns in ways that reinforce people's common conceptions about male and female candidates. To examine the press treatment of men and women candidates, I rely on an extensive content analysis of newspaper coverage.

In addition to documenting gender differences in news coverage, I explore the impact of press patterns on voters' reactions to men and women candidates. An experimental study that replicates the actual patterns of campaign coverage shows how media coverage influences people's perceptions of male and female candidates.

The experimental method also examines voters' stereotypical images of male and female candidates. I look at whether voters depend on stereotypes to distinguish between equivalent male and female candidates and whether these stereotypes influence voters' views. Finally, to see whether the context of the campaign influences the consequences of sex stereotypes, I examine patterns of news coverage and sex stereotyping in gubernatorial and senate campaigns.

With these related data sources—the content analysis of candidates' political advertisements, the content analysis of news coverage, and the experiments investigating the impact of news coverage and sex stereotypes—I examine how people's sex stereotypes influence conduct and consequences of campaigns for U.S. senator and governor.

Content Analysis of Campaign Advertisements

To see whether male and female candidates employ strategies to complement commonly held stereotypes, I examined the televised political advertisements of U.S. Senate and gubernatorial candidates. I selected for analysis television political advertisements instead of newspaper advertisements, because television ads are considered significantly more effective in swaying voters' opinions and are used much more frequently during statewide and national campaigns (Goldenberg and Traugott 1984; Jacobson 1987; Luntz 1988). Goldenberg and Traugott (1987) report, for example, that more than half of all campaign expenditures in senate races are devoted to the production and placement of television advertisements.

In choosing the sample of campaign advertisements, I looked at races contested between 1983 and 1988. In the case of the U.S. Senate, political commercials were obtained for ten of the sixteen women who ran for election between 1984 and 1986, accounting for a total of eighty-two spot ads.[1] To obtain a sample of advertisements for male candidates, I stratified the population of male senate candidates by status (incumbent, challenger, open-race candidate) and selected a sample of twenty-eight male candidates and 324 corresponding political commercials.

For the gubernatorial races, political commercials were obtained for seven of the ten women running for election between 1983 and 1988, resulting in seventy-five spot ads. As in the case of the senate races, I stratified the population of male gubernatorial candidates by status and selected a sample of twenty-one male candidates and 212 corresponding political commercials.[2]

I relied on research on voting, women and politics, and political advertising to develop the coding instrument for the political advertising analysis.[3] For instance, since men and women may choose to emphasize issues and traits that correspond to their stereotypical strengths, the code sheet measured the amount and substance of issue and trait discussion. In addition, since political commercials differ in structure as well as substance (Kaid and Davidson 1986; Shyles 1984), I looked for gender differences in the style of presentation. I examined a variety of potential differences, including the tone of the advertisements, the frequency of criticisms by the candidate, and the candidate's appearance in the ads.[4]

Content Analysis of Campaign Coverage

Sex stereotypes may not only influence how men and women campaign, they may also affect how candidates are treated by the news media. To see whether the press cover male and female candidates differently, I analyzed the content of newspaper coverage in twenty-six U.S. Senate races and twenty-one gubernatorial races between 1983 and 1988.[5]

In drawing the sample of U.S. Senate races, I divided the population of races into the following seven types:

1. Male Incumbent v. Female Challenger
2. Male Incumbent v. Male Challenger
3. Female Incumbent v. Male Challenger
4. Female Incumbent v. Female Challenger
5. Male v. Male in an Open Race
6. Male v. Female in an Open Race
7. Female v. Female in an Open Race

In addition, since senate races vary dramatically in their competitiveness (Westlye 1991), each type of race was further divided by the level of competitiveness, based on final vote returns. Competitive races were those in which the winner garnered no more than 55 percent of the vote, somewhat competitive races were races where the winner won more than 55 percent but no more than 65 percent of the vote, and noncompetitive races were those where the winner received more than 65 percent of the vote. This categorization yielded twenty-one possible categories of races. For each of the twenty-one cat-

TABLE 2.1
A Comparison of the Population and Sample of Senate Races by Type of Race

	Population	Sample
Male Incumbent v. Female Challenger		
Competitive	2[*]	2
Somewhat Competitive[**]	1	1
Not Competitive	9	3
Male Incumbent v. Male Challenger		
Competitive	15	3
Somewhat Competitive	7	3
Not Competitive	21	3
Female Incumbent v. Male Challenger		
Competitive	1	1
Somewhat Competitive	0	0
Not Competitive	1	1
Female Incumbent v. Female Challenger		
Competitive	0	0
Somewhat Competitive	0	0
Not Competitive	0	0
Male v. Male in an Open Race		
Competitive	5	3
Somewhat Competitive	1	1
Not Competitive	2	2
Male v. Female in an Open Race		
Competitive	2[*]	2
Somewhat Competitive	0	0
Not Competitive	0	0
Female v. Female in an Open Race		
Competitive	0	0
Somewhat Competitive	0	0
Not Competitive	1	1
Total	68	26

[*] The competitive race with a female candidate from 1982 was included here.
[**] During the data analysis stage, the competitive and somewhat competitive races in the sample were combined.

egories, three races were randomly selected for analysis.[6] The total number of races in the population and the numbers chosen for the sample are shown in table 2.1. This sampling procedure yielded twenty-four senate races—twelve in 1984 and twelve in 1986. To bolster the number of competitive senate contests with female candidates, the sample includes two 1982 senate races in which women were candidates.

TABLE 2.2
A Comparison of the Population and Sample of
Gubernatorial Races by Type of Race

	Population	Sample
Male Incumbent v. Female Challenger		
Competitive	1	1
Not Competitive	2	2
Male Incumbent v. Male Challenger		
Competitive	13	3
Not Competitive	14	4
Female Incumbent v. Male Challenger		
Competitive	2	2
Not Competitive	0	0
Female Incumbent v. Female Challenger		
Competitive	0	0
Not Competitive	0	0
Male v. Male in an Open Race		
Competitive	25	3
Not Competitive	4	2
Male v. Female in an Open Race		
Competitive	3	3
Not Competitive	0	0
Female v. Female in an Open Race		
Competitive	1	1
Not Competitive	0	0
Total	65	21

When selecting the sample of races for governor, I divided the population of races into two levels of competitiveness—not three—since the results of the senate analysis (described in chapter 4) show that coverage in competitive and somewhat competitive races is similar. Second, because the number of women candidates running for governor is sufficiently small during this period, I included the entire population of female gubernatorial candidates in the sample.[7] Table 2.2 presents the sample and population of gubernatorial races available for analysis.

I selected, for analysis, the largest circulating newspaper since these newspapers are read by more potential voters in each state.[8] (See appendix 3 for a listing of the races included in the sample and the corresponding newspapers.) Given their wide readership, these newspapers could have a profound impact on people's perceptions of candidates running for statewide office. However, by choosing the largest newspaper in the state, I may be underrepresenting gender differences in news patterns, since the largest papers may be more professional and less likely to differentiate between male and female candidates in their campaign coverage.

The content analysis of news coverage began on September 1, the traditional start of the general election campaign.[9] For each day between September 1 and election day, I analyzed all articles that mentioned either candidate, regardless of the article's location in the newspaper. These articles included news articles, columns, editorials, and "news analysis" articles.

I chose to analyze newspaper coverage for both substantive and practical reasons. On the substantive side, there is considerable evidence that newspapers carry more information about state level campaigns than does local television news (Goldenberg and Traugott 1987; Westlye 1991) and that people receive more information about statewide races from newspapers than from television (Clarke and Fredin 1978). In addition, as Westlye (1991) explains, "newspapers present an amount of information that more closely approximates what campaigns are issuing" as compared with local broadcast news (Westlye 1991:45). On the practical side, newspapers are routinely saved on microfilm, thereby making them easily accessible for analysis. In contrast, tapes of local television news are seldom available after a campaign, which makes the examination of television news much more difficult.

In developing a coding scheme for the analysis of newspaper coverage, I relied on findings from the following three areas: electoral politics, media and politics, and women in politics. As an example, we know that people believe that male and female candidates are competent in alternative issues areas. If reporters hold these same stereotypes, then reporters may emphasize different types of issues when covering the campaigns of men and women. For instance, reporters may ask women candidates their positions on health care reform, while they may question male candidates about their plans to balance the budget. To examine whether the press distinguish between male and female candidates in their issue coverage, the content analysis assessed the substance of issue coverage in senate campaigns.

Similarly, I analyzed news characteristics known to be significant for a candidate's electoral success (e.g., amount and prominence of coverage, tone of coverage). For instance, we know that people's evaluations of a candidate's viability can influence their overall evaluations of the candidate and, ultimately, their voting decisions. Because newspeople may view female candidates as less viable than male candidates, the discussion of a female candidate's viability may be more extensive (and more negative) than that of her male counterpart. To explore this possible gender difference in news coverage, the content analysis measured the amount of horse race coverage each candidate received, as well as the press's assessment of the candidate's viability.[10]

Experiments Assessing the Impact of Stereotypes in Campaigns

Voters' perceptions of men and women candidates will be affected by the candidates' behavior as well as the news media's portrayal of the campaign. In addition, voters are likely to consider their own stereotypical views of men and women when casting their ballots. People who view women as more compassionate, for example, may assume that women candidates running for office will be more competent than men at handling "compassion" issues such as health care or child care. Given the pervasiveness of sex stereotypes, people's preconceptions about the strengths and weaknesses of men and women candidates may influence their evaluations of competing candidates.

To see whether gender differences in press coverage and voters' sex stereotypes influence people's perceptions of male and female candidates, I conducted a series of experiments.[11] The experimental method is ideally suited to study these questions because there is a greater degree of control available than with alternative designs, such as surveys or field studies. In the experiment, the investigator intrudes upon nature to provide authoritative answers to causal questions (Kinder and Palfrey 1993).

Two distinct elements of control enable experiments to provide important insights into causal effects. First, by creating experimental conditions, the investigator holds all extraneous factors constant and makes sure that participants encounter stimuli that differ only in theoretically important ways. Second, by assigning participants randomly to treatment conditions, the experimenter can be confident that observed differences between the participants are caused by differences in the treatment conditions. Since proper randomization ensures that participants in the various conditions begin the experiment as approximately equivalent, group differences in the attitudes and behavior of respondents at the end of the experiment must be due to the experimental stimulus.

By creating treatment conditions, the experimenter is able to isolate one causal variable at a time. This control, coupled with randomly assigning participants to experimental conditions, allows the investigator to disentangle complex phenomena into single factors and to examine how each factor influences participants. By isolating one causal agent and controlling for all rival elements, experiments provide important insights regarding causality.

The experimental method is uniquely suited to assess the impact of sex stereotypes and gender differences in media coverage on people's impressions of male and female candidates. By designing an experiment, we can disentangle the impact of gender differences in press patterns from the impact of voters' sex stereotypes. In the real world, distinguishing between these two factors is impossible since they are naturally tied together. That is, women candidates are covered as women candidates, and male candidates are covered as male candidates. Given the perfect covariation between the news media's coverage of men and women and the gender of the candidate in a natural setting, disentangling the impact of these two factors is unachievable with less obtrusive measures.

In contrast, an experiment allows us to differentiate between the effects of coverage patterns and stereotypes by creating the conditions of interest. The experiment, unlike other methods, enables us to measure the independent and cumulative impact of coverage patterns and sex stereotypes on people's perceptions of men and women candidates.

Overview of Experiments

I conducted two sets of experiments investigating the impact of gender differences in campaign coverage and the candidate's sex on people's evaluations of statewide candidates. The first set of experiments, conducted in Ann Arbor, Michigan, in fall 1988, concentrated on evaluations of U.S. Senate candidates. The second series of experiments, conducted in Tempe, Arizona, in summer 1991, examined evaluations of gubernatorial candidates.

In the experiments I used the findings from the content analysis of press patterns to simulate news coverage in an experimental setting. Actual differences in press coverage of men and women, based on the content analysis findings, are recreated in the experimental setting, thereby enabling us to see how real differences in press coverage influence voters' evaluations of men and women candidates.

In addition to examining the influence of news coverage, the experiments allow us to examine whether voters rely on sex stereotypes when evaluating male and female candidates. By varying only the gender of the candidate, we can see whether people use sex stereotypes to distinguish between identical male and female candidates.

By manipulating the type of coverage and the candidates' sex in the experiment, we isolate these two variables and examine their independent and joint impact on evaluations of statewide candidates. First, by holding the candidates' gender constant and manipulating only the type of news coverage, we can determine whether actual gender differences in news presentations influence people's perceptions of the candidates. Second, by holding coverage constant and altering only the candidates' gender, we can see whether people rely on sex stereotypes to draw distinctions between equivalent male and female candidates. Finally, by allowing both the type of coverage and the candidates' gender to vary, we can find out whether both news coverage *and* the sex of the candidate cumulatively affect people's evaluations of male and female candidates.

Experimental Procedure

The advertisements announcing the experiments described them as studies investigating the relationship between the media and politics. Each experiment followed the same basic design. Participants from two local communities came to a research setting at a major university campus. Upon arrival, participants were asked to read a copy of a newspaper page containing several articles. One of these articles, about a statewide campaign, represented the experimental stimulus. The assignment of participants to the experimental conditions was random and was determined by the newspaper page received by the participant. Although participants read different campaign articles representing the various conditions, participants believed they were all reading the same newspaper page.

After the participants finished reading the newspaper page, they were asked to complete a questionnaire. The questionnaire contained general questions about politics, questions about the nonstimulus articles, and a series of questions ascertaining voters' reactions to the candidate described in the campaign article. After completing the questionnaire, participants were given more detail about the purpose of the study, and their questions about the experimental procedure were answered.

Recruitment of Participants

Participants in the experiments were recruited through notices in local newspapers and through posters displayed in public locations in the Ann Arbor/Ypsilanti area and the Phoenix metropolitan area. The notices promised eight dollars for participation in a university sponsored "Media and Politics" study. When volunteers responded to the advertisements by telephone, information about their demographic characteristics was obtained as a way of excluding students and citizens under the age of eighteen. The screening of the applicants over the telephone also helped ensure the proper representation of certain demographic groups (e.g., gender, education level). At the end of the phone interview, participants were assigned to one of several study sessions. Sessions were offered during the day, in the evenings, and on weekends to accommodate people with widely varying work schedules.

Enhancing the Generalizability of the Experimental Results

While experiments are uniquely suited for measuring causality, the generalizability of experiments is sometimes suspect (Campbell and Stanley 1966). One common threat to the generalizability of experiments is the dependence on convenient subject pools (Kinder and Palfrey 1993). In particular, most experimental studies in psychology and political science are conducted with college students. However, college students differ dramatically from typical adult Americans, which hampers the external validity of many experiments.

Since I am interested in seeing whether sex stereotypes and coverage differences influence typical Americans' reactions to men and women candidates, I avoided the easily available sample of college sophomores. The reliance on college students, especially when studying sex stereotypes, is problematic, since students may have more progressive attitudes toward women candidates. In addition, all prior research looking at the impact of sex stereotypes on people's views of political candidates has relied on student samples (e.g., Adams 1975; Ekstrand and Eckert 1981; Mend, Bell, and Bath 1976; Sapiro 1981–1982; Sigelman and Sigelman 1984; Spohn and Gillespie 1987), thereby limiting our understanding of the effect of stereotypes on older and less educated citizens.

For this study I recruited a more diverse group of participants by advertising for volunteers in two distinct communities (Ann Arbor and Tempe). In the Ann Arbor study of senate candidates, 117 individuals participated. Forty percent of the sample was male and sixty percent was female. The mean age of the participants in the sample was 37.3 years old, and the mean education level was 15.3 years. The Tempe study of gubernatorial candidates included 218 individuals with an equal number of males and females participating (109 and 108, respectively). The mean age of the Tempe participants was 38.3 years old, and the mean education level was 15.8 years. The data in table 2.3, a description

TABLE 2.3
Demographic and Political Profile of Experimental Subjects

	Senate (Ann Arbor)	Governor (Tempe)
Sex		
Male	40%	50%
Female	60%	50%
Age		
Mean	37.3	38.3
Range	18–77	18–73
Education		
Mean	15.3	15.8
Range	8–21	8–21
Income		
$14,999 or below	28%	23%
$15,000–$29,999	26%	35%
$30,000–$49,999	32%	30%
$50,000 or above	14%	12%
Party Identification		
Democrat	41%	23%
Independent	33%	35%
Republican	20%	30%
No Preference	6%	12%
Interest in Politics		
Very Interested	45%	35%
Somewhat Interested	44%	54%
Not Very Interested	11%	11%
	(n=117)	(n=218)

of the demographic and political profile of the participants, show that the respondents came from diverse backgrounds. Although this is not a representative sample of the nation, it is a varied sample of two local communities.

Another potential limitation of experiments is the artificial nature of the setting. Because the laboratory setting differs from the real world, participants' reactions to the experimental stimulus may be exaggerated or reduced in an experimental setting (Kinder and Palfrey 1993). Given this threat to the external validity of the experiment, I took several steps to enhance the realism of the study. First, in order to obtain candid responses from participants, the experiments were constructed in such a way that participants were unaware of what was expected of them. The questionnaires included a set of filler questions about governmental policy and national political figures to ensure that participants were unclear about the purpose of each experiment. In addition, participants were provided with a cover story at the start of the experimental session that explained that the purpose of the study was to examine the relationship between politics and the news media. At the end of the experiment, the participants were asked to report what they believed was the purpose of the experiment. The vast majority of the participants (94% in the senate study and 96% in the governor study) simply reported the cover story, which suggests that most of the participants were unaware of the study's true purpose.

To improve the generalizability of the study, I also increased the realistic nature of the experimental stimulus. First, with a desktop publishing program, I created a newspaper page that looked like an actual page from a newspaper, so participants believed that they were reading about an authentic candidate. Second, a reporter was hired to edit the campaign articles so that they read as though they were genuine newspaper articles. The reporter, when editing the articles, relied on the stylistic rules prescribed in *The Associated Press Stylebook and Libel Manual.*

Finally, the realism of the study was enhanced by relying on the content analysis of news coverage to create the experimental stimulus. The articles that participants read were not merely fictional articles. Instead, participants read prototypical articles representing authentic differences in the news media's coverage of men and women candidates for statewide office.

To examine how stereotypes influence the effectiveness of political campaigns, I look at the candidates' political advertisements and campaign coverage in gubernatorial and U.S. Senate elections. In addition, I simulate the substance of the campaign in an experimental setting to see how the press coverage of campaigns, as well as the candidates' gender, influence voters' perceptions of men and women candidates. Finally, by looking at two distinct electoral settings (races for senator and governor), I can determine whether the context of the campaign influences the consequences of sex stereotyping. In the next chapter I begin by looking at a campaign setting that emphasizes women's stereotypical weaknesses: the U.S. Senate.

3

Gender Differences in Campaign Appeals for the U.S. Senate

☼

The consequences that stereotypes have in political campaigns depend on the prevailing electoral climate. When the salient issues in a campaign correspond to a woman candidate's stereotypical strengths, women will be aided by people's stereotypes. In contrast, when the prominent policy concerns overlap with a woman candidate's perceived weaknesses, women will be in a less enviable position. In the 1980s, women running for the U.S. Senate faced a daunting political environment. The United States and the Soviet Union were still in the midst of the cold war, making foreign policy and defense issues especially prominent. In addition, because of the ballooning budget and rising interest rates, economic issues were on the minds of most voters. This constellation of issues played to women's perceived weaknesses, thereby potentially handicapping women in their campaigns for the U.S. Senate.

In this chapter I look at how a hostile political environment affects the campaigns of men and women for the U.S. Senate. In particular, I examine how the stereotypical images that voters, journalists, and campaign strategists carry around "in their heads" influence the strategies adopted by candidates. To examine whether a candidate's choice of campaign strategy conforms to commonly held stereotypes, I examine the political commercials of candidates running for U.S. senator between 1982 and 1986.[1]

The substance of political commercials is completely controlled by the candidate and the candidate's staff. These ads, therefore, represent the candidate's presentation of self (Kaid and Davidson 1986). Looking at the content of these ads enables us to see whether men and women conceptualize their candidacies differently. If male and female candidates adopt distinct strategies in their electoral bids, these differences may lead to gender differences in the effectiveness of their campaigns. In other words, by employing alternative campaign appeals, male and female candidates could be adopting appeals that differ in their impact on voters. Since political advertisements have the power to influence voters' perceptions of candidates, thereby influencing voting decisions (e.g., Joslyn 1984; Kern 1989; Patterson and McClure 1976), an examination of political advertisements has important electoral implications.

In addition, by comparing the content of spot advertisements with news coverage of the candidates, we can look at differences in the news media's responsiveness to the messages of men and women candidates. The candidates' campaign themes, as presented in their ads, will be most coherent and effective if these themes are echoed by the press. If the agendas of the candidates and the news media do not correspond, then the impact of the candidates' messages may be blunted. Furthermore, systematic differences in how well the news media represent the campaigns of men and women may signal bias by the news media.

Gender Differences in the Style of Presentation

When candidates are developing their political advertising strategy, they need to consider what message they will present to the public and how this message will be delivered. Decisions about both the substance and the structure of commercials are likely to be influenced by the public's stereotypical images of men and women. For instance, when candidates are creating their political commercials, they need to decide whether to appear in their own ads or whether to rely on a spokesperson to deliver their message. When making this decision, political strategists are likely to recognize that women candidates are perceived as more honest than male candidates. Given this stereotype, women candidates are likely to be featured more prominently in their own commercials, since trustworthy spokespeople are clearly more persuasive (Milburn 1991).

In the 1980s women senate candidates were more likely than their male counterparts to appear in their own ads.[2] Women candidates appeared in 87 percent of their commercials, while men were present in 79 percent of their advertisements.[3] While these differences are not dramatic, they are consistent: women senate candidates, regardless of their status, were more likely than their male counterparts to deliver their own campaign messages.

Stereotypes about men and women are also related to *how* candidates appear in their campaign commercials. When appearing in their campaign commercials, candidates often alternate between formal attire (e.g., business suit) and more informal apparel (e.g., jeans, sweaters). By promoting a more eclectic appearance, candidates hope to widen their appeals. Voters may view the formally dressed candidate as professional and experienced, while the same candidate dressed more casually is likely to be viewed as warm and compassionate.

While varying the candidates' attire is a way of broadening their appeal, such a strategy is not open to women candidates who must convince voters of their legitimacy and professionalism. Perhaps because of their novelty, women candidates feel a need to stress the seriousness of their candidacy by dressing in a professional manner. The data in figure 3.1 show that women are much more likely than their male counterparts to dress formally in their campaign

FIGURE 3.1   *Percentage of Commercials Where Senate Candidate Appears in Formal Attire*

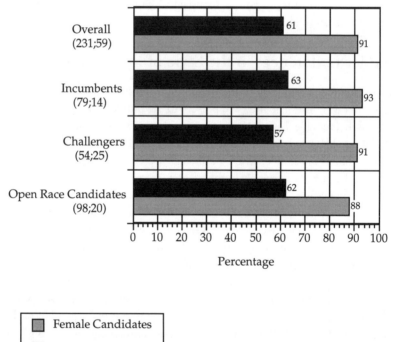

Note: In each comparison, the difference between male and female candidates is statistically significant at p < .10. The p value is based on the difference in proportions test. The number in parentheses is the number of commercials examined for male candidates followed by the number of commercials examined for female candidates for each type of candidate.

commercials. This gender difference in attire is remarkably stable, holding for all types of senate candidates—incumbents, challengers, and candidates in open races.

Women wear professional attire, like business suits, in more than 90 percent of their ads, while men dress formally only about 60 percent of the time. For example, Millicent Fenwick of New Jersey wore dark suits in each of her commercials in her 1982 bid for the U.S. Senate. Her opponent, Frank Lautenberg, on the other hand, aired advertisements where he appeared without a tie or jacket when speaking informally with potential supporters on street corners and in a local mall.

People's stereotypes about men and women also affect the effectiveness of positive and negative appeals for men and women candidates. Trent and Friedenberg (1983) explain that since women are viewed as less assertive than men, they are expected to be less verbally aggressive in their electoral campaigns. Therefore when women violate these expectations by initiating aggressive and forceful attacks, they are viewed negatively (Wadsworth, Patterson, Kaid, Cullers, Malcomb, and Lamirand 1987). In particular, voters view women candidates who initiate aggressive attacks as "unfeminine, shrill, [and] vicious" (p. 115).[4] In their experimental study of television advertising in the 1990 California gubernatorial campaign, Ansolabehere and Iyengar (1991) provide empirical support for this contention. In particular, Ansolabehere and Iyengar find that "attack" ads were significantly less effective for Diane Feinstein than for Pete Wilson.

Given people's preconceptions regarding "proper" female behavior, negative advertisements are likely to be especially problematic for women candidates. However, women candidates for the U.S. Senate often air negative commercials during their campaigns. If fact, women senate candidate use "attack" ads significantly more often than their male counterparts, even within status categories (i.e., female challengers employ negative advertisements more frequently than male challengers). Women senate candidates use negative appeals 46 percent of the time, while their male colleagues choose negative ads only 32 percent of the time.[5]

Women senate candidates, in addition to airing more negative advertisements, are more likely than other candidates to appear in their negative ads. For instance, female senatorial candidates appear in 88 percent of their negative commercials, while their male counterparts appear only 70 percent of the time.[6] According to many campaign consultants, by appearing in their own negative ads, candidates run the risk of being mistakenly associated with the problem that they are attacking (Kern 1989). Women senate candidates, by airing and appearing in negative commercials, are adopting a campaign strategy that is likely to weaken their candidacy.

Finally, when deciding whether to engage in negative campaigning, candidates consider their opponents' gender. Lake (1984), in her interviews with male and female congressional candidates, finds that men feel uncomfortable when their campaigns attack female opponents. Male candidates believe that if they engage in a negative campaign they will be perceived as "beating up on" women. The male candidates' apprehension about attacking female opponents is documented in the candidates' advertisements. Men use attack ads against male opponents 35 percent of the time, while they employ these negative advertisements only 15 percent of the time when facing female opponents.[7]

Gender Differences in the Substance of Political Commercials

People's preconceptions about the typical characteristics of men and women candidates also affect the topics that candidates choose to highlight in their campaigns. To begin, a candidate's gender can affect whether a candidate makes a personal or a policy-oriented appeal to the electorate. Because people believe that women are less competent than men, female candidates may feel a need to emphasize policy concerns in their campaign commercials. By talking about their issue priorities, women candidates hope to dispel voters' doubts about their ability. Male candidates, on the other hand, can be more flexible in their appeals, since voters are more confident about their candidacies.

The commercials of the candidates show that women are only somewhat more likely than men to emphasize issues in their commercials. More than three-quarters (76%) of the women candidates' advertisements mention issues while male candidates discuss policy in 71 percent of their ads.[8] This difference in issue discussion is most pronounced among incumbents, with gender differences in policy emphasis disappearing among challengers and candidates in open issues.

Furthermore, both men and women focus more extensively on their issue priorities while spending significantly less time discussing their personal characteristics. Almost three-fourths of all the commercials in the sample discuss the candidates' issue concerns while fewer than half of the ads focus on the candidates' personality traits. For example, 74 percent of the senate commercials discuss substantive issues, while 40 percent of the ads mention the candidates' personal strengths. Even within status categories, candidates prefer to focus on policy rather than personality in their commercials.

Issues in Campaign Commercials

Although issues are discussed extensively in campaign commercials, candidates rarely take controversial policy stands in these advertisements. Instead, candidates typically talk in general terms about the issues that they consider important. This type of issue discussion is not trivial. On the contrary, campaign ads offer voters a view of a candidate's issue priorities, thereby playing an agenda-setting role in campaigns.[9]

People's stereotypes about male and female candidates are likely to influence the types of issues that candidates choose to emphasize in their campaign appeals. Since voters' priorities about issues are responsive to the media's emphasis, candidates try to influence these priorities during their campaigns by emphasizing their stereotypical strengths. More specifically, by stressing their perceived strengths in their advertisements, candidates are attempting to make these issues more salient to voters, thereby leading voters to consider these issues when evaluating the competing candidates.

Given this campaign strategy, women are likely to concentrate on "female" issues, such as education and health policy, while men are more likely to stress their commitment to "male" issues, such as the economy and defense policy.[10] By stressing these alternative domains, male and female candidates are trying to "prime" issues that will uniquely benefit their own candidacies.

Of course, men and women may articulate alternative agendas for other than strategic reasons. More specifically, gender differences in issue emphasis could reflect real differences in the issue priorities of male and female candidates. Research examining the political attitudes of women officeholders suggests that men and women in the U.S. House and state legislatures emphasize markedly different agendas during their tenure in office (Carroll, Dodson, and Mandel 1992; Kathlene, Clarke, and Fox 1991; Poole and Zeigler 1985; Thomas 1991). For instance, Carroll, Dodson, and Mandel (1992), examining a national representative sample of men and women in state legislatures, show that women are more likely than men to sponsor legislation concerning day care, the elderly, health care, and education. These differences in legislative priorities persist even when controlling for the party of the candidate.

The data in figure 3.2 show that men and women do emphasize alternative agendas in their campaigns. Male candidates focus on their stereotypical strengths by discussing economic issues and foreign affairs in their commercials, while female candidates emphasize their own stereotypical strengths when they stress social programs and social issues in their controlled communications. For instance, in Senate Paula Hawkins's 1986 reelection campaign in Florida, she highlighted her efforts to help abused and missing children by explaining that she had laid the groundwork for a law that enlarged the federal government's role in finding missing children. In contrast, John Kerry stressed war and peace issues in his 1984 Massachusetts senate campaign. During the campaign, Kerry

FIGURE 3.2   *The Discussion of Issues in Senate Commercials*

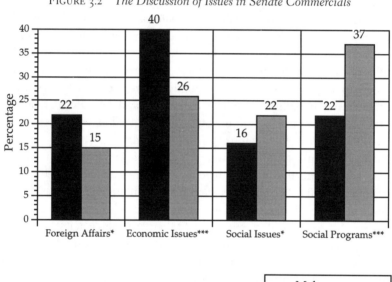

Note: The "foreign affairs" category includes discussion of the following: USSR-U.S. relations, arms control, Central America, South Africa, the Middle East, and Europe. The "economic issues" category includes discussion of the following: taxes, the federal budget, and discussion of the economy generally. The "social issues" category includes the discussion of gay rights, abortion, school prayer, women's rights, civil rights, the environment, and drugs. The "social program" category includes discussion of education, health programs, employment, welfare programs, and programs for the elderly. For male candidates, the percentage of issue discussion was based on 324 issue mentions in the commercials; for female candidates, the percentage of issue discussion was based on 82 issue mentions in the commercials.
*** p<.01
** p<.05
* p<.10

repeatedly criticized his opponent, Raymond Shamie, for his support of President Reagan's military buildup and policies in Central America.

These results suggest that in their campaigns for the U.S. Senate, male candidates are adopting a strategy that emphasizes traditionally relevant issues such as foreign policy and economics. Women candidates, on the other hand, are trying to alter the typical agenda by highlighting their concern for less traditional issues; this latter strategy is probably more difficult and may be less effective.

Personal Traits in Political Commercials

Besides demonstrating their concern for issues, candidates also illustrate their personal strengths in their commercials. Scholars of voting behavior have identified two major dimensions of trait evaluation: competence and integrity (Markus 1982; Miller, Wattenberg, and Malanchuk 1986). The competence dimension is defined by traits such as "knowledge," "leadership," "experience," and "intelligence," while the integrity dimension is defined by "honesty," "morality," and "trustworthiness." With these dimensions in mind, we can examine the substance of trait discussion to see whether men and women differ in what personality traits they highlight in their campaign messages.

People's stereotypes about the personality strengths of male and female candidates influence the traits that candidates stress in their commercials. Since voters consider women candidates to be more compassionate and honest, while they consider men stronger leaders and more knowledgeable, candidates develop campaign strategies to accent or revise these stereotypes. As with issues, candidates may choose to emphasize their perceived personality strengths in their campaign commercials. Benze and DeClerq (1985) find support for this hypothesis in their study of political commercials. In their research Benze and DeClerq compare the content of 113 political advertisements for male and female House and Senate candidates and find that male candidates emphasize their toughness three times as often as female candidates. Similarly, female candidates stress their compassion and warmth twice as often as their male counterparts.

However, this strategy of emphasizing stereotypical personality traits is likely to be problematic for women candidates. While the public's issue agenda is susceptible to media influence, people's perceptions of important personality characteristics is less flexible. Research at the presidential level suggests that assessments of a candidate's competence and leadership are more influential than other trait assessments (e.g., Markus 1982; Miller, Wattenberg, and Malanchuk

1986). Similarly, Rosenwasser and Dean's (1989) research shows that students rate tough and aggressive traits as more important than warm and expressive traits when asked to assess the qualities of a "good" politician. Furthermore, the possession of typical masculine traits appears to increase a candidate's perceived competence across a variety of different issues (Huddy and Terkildsen 1993), while typical feminine personality traits, such as compassion and empathy, are considered less important for office holders (e.g., Huddy 1994; Kinder 1986).

Given the greater importance assigned to "male" traits relative to "female" traits, it is probably worthwhile for both men and women candidates to empha- size "male" traits in their campaign appeals.[11] Men can highlight their stereo- typical strengths, while women will want to eradicate stereotypes by stressing "male" traits in their own campaign appeals.

The data in table 3.1 indicate that women are trying to revise potentially damaging stereotypes by focusing on their competence much more heavily than their male counterparts. Overall, women mention their competence in 32 percent of their commercials, while men focus on their competence in less than one-quarter (18%) of their commercials. This gender difference in the discussion of traits occurs for all types of candidates—incumbents, chal- lengers, and candidates in open races.

Finally, the data in table 3.1 show that, regardless of the candidates' gen- der, candidates emphasize their competence more than any other personal characteristic. According to recent research on voting behavior, this empha- sis is well founded. For instance, in his study of the 1980 presidential elec- tion, Markus (1982) found that assessments of competence had a much

TABLE 3.1
The Discussion of Personality Traits in Senate Commercials[1]

	Senate Candidates	
	Men	Women
Competence[2]	18%[a]	32%[a]
Compassion	5%	3%
Industriousness	4%	0%
Integrity	5%	8%
Strength/Toughness	3%	7%
Aggressiveness	5%	3%
	(324 ads; 28 candidates)[3]	(82 ads; 10 candidates)

[1] Cells sharing superscripts are significantly different from each other at p<.05. The p value is based on the difference in proportions test.
[2] The "competence" category includes discussion of the following: experience, knowledge, leadership, intelligence. The "integrity" category includes discussion of the following: honesty, morality, trustworthiness.
[3] For each column, entries are the number of ads on which the percentages are based, followed by the num- ber of candidates represented in the ads.

more powerful effect on overall evaluations of a candidate than assessments of integrity.

The examination of campaign commercials suggests that male and female candidates campaign differently for statewide office. These differences include how the candidates appear in their ads, what they choose to talk about, and whether they adopt a negative or a positive campaign. These differences appear to be driven by the unique constraints that men and women face in the electoral arena. However, there is some overlap in the strategies employed by men and women. For instance, all candidates, regardless of their gender, prefer to talk about policy over personality in their advertisements; when they do highlight their personality strengths, candidates stress their competence more often than any other trait.

The Correspondence Between Campaign Advertisements and News Coverage

The results of the political advertising analysis demonstrate that men and women articulate different agendas in their electoral bids and these alternative agendas correspond to people's stereotypical beliefs. Candidates probably adopt these strategies because they believe these appeals will be most effective in garnering votes. However, these strategies will be most influential when the messages are reinforced and echoed by the news media. In particular, voters are more likely to learn about a specific campaign message if they are exposed to this message repeatedly during the campaign—through "uncontrolled" (i.e., news) and "controlled" (i.e., ads) media sources.

While men and women stress different campaign themes, the news media may not be equally responsive to their messages. Reporters, like their readers, may have stereotypical beliefs that influence the substance of their campaign coverage. In addition, stereotypes could lead reporters to consider male candidates more "legitimate"; consequently, reporters may echo male candidates' campaign rhetoric more faithfully.

On the other hand, differences in the correspondence between the press's and the candidates' messages may reflect real differences in the campaign abilities of men and women candidates. If male candidates, for example, are more effective campaigners than their female counterparts, then they will have an easier time influencing the media's agenda. If this is the case, the news media may be responding to the ability of the candidates and not to their gender.

Yet, regardless of the cause, gender differences in the correspondence between the press's agenda and the candidates' agendas have important electoral consequences. Since voters' priorities are flexible and susceptible to media influence, candidates who can dominate the media's agenda will be more successful in influencing the public's agenda. These candidates, who will presumably emphasize their strengths in their campaign appeals, may have an easier time winning election.

The data in table 3.2 reinforce earlier findings by showing that men and women senate candidates emphasize their traditional strengths in their campaign appeals.[12] By stressing these issues the candidates hope to generate more support for their candidacies. However, the data also demonstrate that the news media are more responsive to the male candidates' agendas. Male candidates for the U.S. Senate focus on "male" issues 73 percent of the time, and this emphasis is clearly echoed by the news media, who discuss "male" issues 71 percent of the time. Female senate candidates, on the other hand, concentrate on "female" issues, discussing these policies 59 percent of the time. The news media ignore this focus, however, and discuss "female" issues only 46 percent of the time.

The media's greater responsiveness to the agenda of male candidates is not simply a reflection of status differences. Regardless of the candidates' status, the news media in senate races represent the agenda of male candidates more accurately. For example, in races for open senate seats, men mention "male" issues in 74 percent of their ads, and they devote 66 percent of their issue coverage to these issues. For female senate candidates in open seats, there is con-

TABLE 3.2

Comparison of "Male" and "Female" Issue Emphasis in Spot Ads and in News Coverage in Senate Races[1]

	Male Candidates		Female Candidates	
	News Coverage	Spot Ads	News Coverage	Spot Ads
"Male" Issues[2]	71%[a]	73%[b]	54%[ac]	41%[bc]
"Female" Issues	29%	27%	46%	59%
	(6624; 25)[3]	(283; 25)	(1303; 7)	(69; 7)

[1] Cells sharing superscripts are significantly different from each other. The p value is based on the difference in proportions test.

[2] "Male" issues include foreign policy, defense spending, arms control, foreign trade, farm issues, and the economy; "female" issues include day care, helping the poor, education, health care, women's rights, drug abuse, and the environment.

[3] For each column, entries are the number of "male" and "female" issue mentions coded, followed by the number of candidates.

[a,b] $p<.01$

[c] $p<.05$

siderable incongruity between the candidates' and the media's message. While women focus on "female" issues almost two-thirds of the time (64%), less than half (47%) of the issue coverage by the media is devoted to "female" issues.

Men and women not only emphasize distinct issues in their campaigns for statewide office, they also stress different personality characteristics. In particular, women are more likely than their male counterparts to emphasize their competence and experience in their campaign communications. Yet, as is the case with issue coverage, the news media do not represent the unique agenda of women candidates.

As the data in table 3.3 indicate, the news media accurately reflect the trait emphasis of male candidates, while largely ignoring the trait emphasis of women candidates. The correspondence between what the candidates say and what the news media report is almost perfect for male candidates, while there is a substantially weaker correspondence for women candidates. As with issues, this gender difference in media correspondence is not a reflection of status differences between men and women candidates. For example, male challengers in senate races stress "male" traits 67 percent of the time in their ads, and these traits are covered in the news 72 percent of the time. In contrast, female challengers discuss "male" traits almost exclusively in their ads—91 percent of the time. But these same traits receive much less attention by the news media; less than half (41%) of all trait discussion is devoted to "male" traits.

These results suggest that the news media are more receptive to the messages of male candidates. When covering male candidates, reporters emphasize the same personality traits and policy areas as the candidates. News coverage of female candidates is much less responsive; there is considerable

TABLE 3.3
Comparison of "Male" and "Female" Trait Emphasis in Spot Ads and in News Coverage in Senate Races[1]

	Male Candidates		Female Candidates	
	News Coverage	Spot Ads	News Coverage	Spot Ads
"Male" Issues[2]	70%[a]	71%[b]	55%[ac]	78%[bc]
"Female" Issues	30%	29%	45%	22%
	(1090; 25)[3]	(121; 25)	(1303; 7)	(28; 7)

[1] Cells sharing superscripts are significantly different from each other. The p value is based on the difference in proportions test.
[2] "Male" traits include the following: independence, knowledge, objectivity, strong leadership, toughness; "female" traits include honesty, sensitivity, gentleness, and compassion.
[3] For each column, entries are the number of "male" and "female" trait mentions coded, followed by the number of candidates.
[a,b] p<.01
[c] p<.05

incongruity between what the candidates say and what the press report. By accurately mirroring the campaign rhetoric of male candidates and distorting the rhetoric of female candidates, the news media blunt the effectiveness of women candidates' campaign strategies.

This analysis of the political advertisements in thirty-eight senate campaigns suggests that male and female candidates adopt campaign strategies that are remarkably similar in certain dimensions and strikingly different in others. First, in their advertisements both male and female candidates prefer to talk about policy over personality. In addition, when personality traits are discussed, both men and women stress their competence more than any other trait.

In addition to these similarities, the examination of political commercials illustrates a series of differences in the way that men and women campaign for statewide office. These differences in campaign appeals appear to be driven by the unique electoral constraints faced by male and female candidates. Candidates differ in how they appear in their ads, in what topics they choose to talk about, and in whether they adopt positive or negative campaigns. Women, for example, almost always dress professionally in their commercials, while men are about as likely to dress casually as formally. In addition, male candidates are more likely to stress economic issues in their campaigns, while women spend more time emphasizing their commitment to social issues. Similarly, women candidates are more likely than their male counterparts to stress their experience and leadership ability.

While men and women articulate alternative agendas as a way of increasing support for their candidacies, the news media are more responsive to the messages of male candidates. The news media's agenda almost mirrors that issued by male candidates in their televised political advertisements. Reporters emphasize the same personality traits and the policy areas as male candidates, while largely ignoring the alternative agenda articulated by women candidates.

The news media's unresponsiveness to female candidates' campaign agendas can dampen those candidates' electoral prospects. Women are likely to adopt different strategies than their male counterparts because they believe these strategies will be more effective for their unique candidacies. Yet, by failing to represent the alternative agenda of women candidates, the news media is limiting the effectiveness of women's campaign strategies. By muting the campaign messages of women candidates, the press is likely to hamper women in their quest for seats in the U.S. Senate.

4

Differences in Campaign Coverage: An Examination of U.S. Senate Races

❈

In the preceding chapter I demonstrated that candidates consider people's stereotypical images of their candidacy when choosing campaign themes in their electoral contests. In addition, the comparison of the candidates' commercials with the coverage of the candidates in the news indicated that the news media is much more likely to mirror the campaign messages issued by male candidates. In this chapter, I look more extensively at the news media's treatment of men and women senate candidates to see whether the press reinforce stereotypes in their coverage. If the press differentiate between men and women candidates, this treatment could influence voters' overall impressions of the candidates, thereby influencing the candidates chances of election to the Senate

Gender Differences in News Coverage of Male and Female Senate Candidates

The news media may cover male and female candidates differently for a number of reasons. First, gender differences in coverage could reflect stereotypes newspeople hold about male and female candidates. Since stereotypes are pervasive and cut across education and occupation lines, reporters and editors are likely to embrace them. For instance, journalists may view men as uniquely qualified to deal with certain policy areas, while women are viewed as having expertise in other areas. If this is the case, newspeople are likely to concentrate on alternative policy areas when covering the campaigns of male and female candidates.

Second, the news media may differentiate between men and women candidates in their coverage of U.S. Senate campaigns because newspeople are trying to play to the stereotypical images held by their readers. Reporters, for instance, may not believe that women can handle educational issues better than men. However, they are likely to believe that their readers hold such beliefs and, therefore, they ask women about their position on educational issues as a way of anticipating their readers' interests.

Third, differences in newspaper coverage of male and female senate candidates could be driven by organizational incentives common to news organizations. When covering campaigns reporters and editors rely on standard criteria of newsworthiness (Epstein 1973; Graber 1989), and reliance on these criteria could lead to differences in how newspeople describe the campaigns of men and women in their local newspapers. For instance, because female candidates for the U.S. Senate commonly wage noncompetitive campaigns, their candidacies could be treated as less newsworthy. Consequently, they are likely to receive less coverage and less prominent coverage than their male counterparts.

Finally, gender differences in news coverage could reflect real differences in the campaigns of men and women. As illustrated in chapter 3, male and female candidates often adopt alternative strategies, stressing different themes and issues in their electoral campaigns. For example, in her 1992 bid for the U.S. Senate, Patty Murray stressed her unique female candidacy by describing herself as a "mom in tennis shoes" instead of as a state senator (Congressional Quarterly [1992]:3353). Authentic differences in male and female campaigns can affect how reporters cover races for the U.S. Senate.

This chapter examines newspaper coverage as a way of identifying systematic differences in press treatment of male and female U.S. Senate candidates. I investigate gender differences in the *quantity* and *quality* of press coverage.

Quantity of Media Coverage

Media treatment of male and female candidates can differ in a number of important ways, but one potentially important difference is in the sheer amount of news coverage. Gender differences in the amount of news attention are important, since candidates who receive less attention by the media are less likely to be recognized and less likely to be supported at the polls (Goldenberg and Traugott 1984; Jacobson 1992). The results of the content analysis demonstrate that women candidates consistently receive less press attention than male candidates.[1] As the data in figure 4.1 indicate, 38.4 paragraphs a day are devoted to all-male senate races, while only 29.6 paragraphs a day are written about races including female candidates.[2]

FIGURE 4.1   *Average Number of Paragraphs Published About Senate Races Each Day*

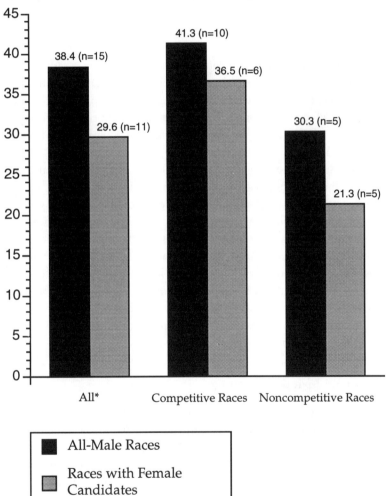

Note: * indicates that the difference in coverage is statistically significant at p < .10 level. The p value is based on the t statistic. The number in parentheses is the number of races examined for each category.

The greater attention given to male candidates does not merely reflect gender differences in the candidates' electoral strength. Races with women candidates consistently receive less news attention, *regardless* of the competitiveness of the contest.[3] Furthermore, gender differences in the amount of coverage are not driven by differences in the size of newspapers in states where men and women compete. More specifically, male candidates are not more likely to run in states where the newspapers are larger: the average newshole[4] for races with male candidates is 4,094 column inches, while the average newshole for female candidate races is almost as large at 3,939 column inches.

Coverage of individual candidates, like coverage of races, varies with the gender of the candidate. Overall, thirteen paragraphs are published about male candidates each day, while only ten paragraphs are devoted to female candidates each day. Although the gender differences in coverage are neither large nor statistically significant, these differences are consistent and occur for competitive and noncompetitive candidates.

These results suggest that journalists hold preconceptions about women candidates that lead them to consider women to be less viable than their male counterparts. Journalists believe that male candidates are likely to wage stronger campaigns than female candidates, and they therefore devote more news space to the male candidates' campaigns. These gender differences in press attention are likely to have electoral consequences. Since less news attention is devoted to women candidates, regardless of their competitiveness, voters will have a difficult time acquiring information about these candidates. Therefore voters will be less familiar with women candidates and may be less willing to support them at the polls. These differences in press attention could threaten women's chances of election to the Senate.

Substance of Media Coverage

News coverage of campaigns not only influences voters' ability to recognize candidates, it also determines the quality of information available to potential voters. By examining the substance of news coverage in Senate elections, we can see what voters are likely to learn during these campaigns and what voters are likely to consider when choosing between competing candidates. If the substance of news coverage varies with the candidates' gender, then the voting calculus used by citizens is likely to differ for male and female candidates.

Horse Race Coverage

Since assessments of a candidate's issue stands, traits, and viability all influence voters' impressions of candidates (e.g., Bartels 1988; Markus and Converse 1979; Kinder and Sears 1985; Markus 1982; Page and Jones 1979; Wright and Berkman 1986), news information about these evaluation dimensions is likely to affect the decisions of voters. With regard to viability, stereotypes held by reporters and editors could lead them to consider women candidates as less viable. As a result, newspeople may focus more intensely on horse race issues (e.g., who is ahead or behind in the polls, who has the strongest campaign organization) when covering women for the Senate.[5]

The results of the content analysis indicate that horse race coverage is more prevalent for female senate candidates than for their male counterparts (see

FIGURE 4.2   *Percentage of Articles Devoted to the Horse Race in Senate Campaigns*

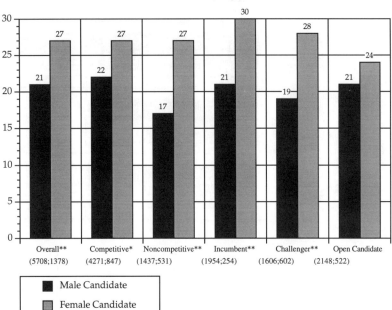

Note: Horse race coverage includes any discussion of a candidate's changes of winning including comparisons of the two candidates' organization, discussion of poll results, or the candidates' performance in campaign debates. The p value is based on the difference in proportions test. The numbers in parentheses are the number of articles on which the percentages are based; the number of articles about male candidates are followed by the number of articles about female candidates.
** p < .01
* p < .05

figure 4.2) Overall, 21 percent of the articles about male candidates discuss the horse race, compared with 27 percent of the articles about female candidate. This greater emphasis on the horse race for female candidates occurs for all types of candidates: competitive and noncompetitive candidates, incumbents, challengers, and candidates in open races.

The news media's emphasis on horse race aspects of political campaigns does have implications for the success of men and women candidates. First, by concentrating on the horse race, the news media will make the women candidates' viability more salient to voters. Second, the focus on the candidates' viability can produce negative assessments of the candidates if the substance of

FIGURE 4.3   *Press Assessments Regarding the Viability of Senate Candidates*

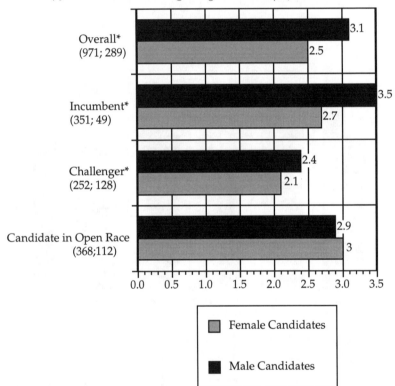

Note: Press viability assessments were rated on a four-point scale where 4 denotes "likely winner," 3 denotes "competitive," 2 denotes "somewhat competitive," and 1 denotes "sure loser." The p value is based on the t statistic. The numbers in parentheses are the number of horse race paragraphs examined for male candidates followed by the number of horse race paragraphs examined for female candidates.
* p < .01

the horse race coverage is negative. To examine the content of horse race coverage, every press assessment of a candidate's viability was rated on a scale from 1 to 4, with 1 indicating "sure loser," 2 indicating "somewhat competitive," 3 indicating "competitive," and 4 indicating "likely winner." As the data in figure 4.3 show, female candidates are consistently described by the press as less viable than their male challengers. Male candidates are usually viewed as competitive by the press (3.1), while female candidates are more likely to be labeled as somewhat less competitive (2.5).

Furthermore, this difference in viability assessments for male and female candidates is not simply a reflection of status differences for male and female candidates. Gender differences in viability assessments occur among challengers and incumbents; female incumbents and female challengers are viewed by the press as less viable than their male colleagues.[6]

Campaign Resources

News attention to campaign resources (e.g., the strength of the candidate's campaign organization, the candidate's fundraising capabilities) is an important element of campaign coverage, since such discussion is likely to contribute to voters' judgments about a candidate's viability. The conventional wisdom (see Carroll 1985 for a description), although lacking empirical support (e.g., Burrell 1985), contends that female candidates are often at a disadvantage with regard to campaign financing. This conventional wisdom appears to affect press treatment of women candidates. According to the content analysis results, negative resources are discussed by the media more frequently for female candidates. Only 5 percent of the articles written about male candidates mention a lack of resources, while twice as many articles (10%) about female candidates discuss their scarcity of resources. These gender differences occur for all women candidates: negative resources are emphasized more often in the coverage of female incumbents, female challengers and females in open races.[7]

The results presented above show that female candidates often receive more horse race coverage than comparable male candidates and that the substance of this coverage is more negative for female candidates. The press's emphasis on the horse race can hinder women in their quest for election, since voters who look to the news media will be given a great deal of information about the electability of women senate candidates and much of this information will highlight the women candidates' unlikely chances of victory.

Issue Coverage

Citizens consider issue positions in addition to viability when evaluating competing candidates for statewide office (e.g., Abramowitz and Segal 1993; Hinckley, Hofstetter, and Kessel 1974; Westlye 1991; Wright and Berkman 1986). Because of its control over campaign information, the press can influence the significance of issues in a number of ways. First, by covering certain policy issues and ignoring others, the media can influence the public's issue priorities during campaigns. Second, and perhaps more important, by emphasizing certain issues, the news media can determine the criteria voters use when evaluating candidates. Finally, newspeople can influence the likelihood of issue voting by controlling the quantity (and quality) of issue information available to potential voters. For example, by presenting detailed discussions of issues in the newspaper, the press encourage voters to use issues when evaluating the candidates. In contrast, if the information about candidates' policy positions is scant, voters will be unlikely to consider issues when casting their votes.

Although men and women senate candidates are equally likely to focus on issues in their campaign commercials, as demonstrated in chapter 3, the press devote significantly more attention to the policy priorities of male candidates. As the data in figure 4.4 show, almost four paragraphs are published about

FIGURE 4.4   *Average Number of Paragraphs Published About Issues in Senate Races Each Day*

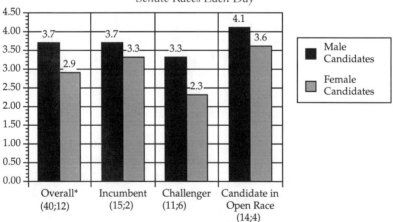

Note: * indicates that the difference in coverage is statistically significant at p < .01. The p value is based on the t statistic. The number in parentheses is the number of races examined for each type of candidate; the number of races with male candidates is followed by the number of races with female candidates.

male candidates' issue positions each day, while fewer than three paragraphs a day are published about the issue priorities of female candidates. The tendency of the press to downplay issue concerns for women candidates is remarkably consistent—gender differences in issue coverage occur for incumbents, challengers, and candidates in open races.[8]

Journalists may spend less time focusing on issues when covering women candidates because viability concerns are so pervasive. Because of the emphasis on the horse race, journalists simply have less time and space to cover the issue concerns of women candidates. Or, holding the same stereotypes as their readers, journalists believe that women are less knowledgeable and therefore consider women candidates' positions on issues to be less newsworthy.

Whatever the reason, readers consistently receive less policy information about women candidates in races for the Senate. This lack of issue attention by the press, coupled with the emphasis on the horse race discussed earlier, could lead voters to discount issues and emphasize viability when developing impressions of female candidates. Voters who are less familiar with the women candidates' positions on issues may be reluctant to support these candidates at the polls. In contrast, issues are likely to play a more central role in the evaluations of male candidates, since issues receive more attention and the horse race less attention in the news coverage of male candidates.

The analysis of the candidates' commercials in chapter 3 demonstrated that men and women articulate alternative issue agendas in their campaigns for the U.S. Senate. Men stress their stereotypical strengths (e.g., economic and foreign policy issues), while women focus on their perceived areas of expertise (e.g., education, health care, poverty). For example, in his 1984 reelection campaign Rudy Boschwitz stressed the need for military parity with the Soviet Union as well as proposing a "fair play" budget to limit increases in all areas of government spending. In contrast, in her 1986 senate race Lt. Governor Harriet Woods of Missouri touted her efforts to reform nursing homes in her public appearances and in her political advertisements.

The comparison of the news and advertising data, based on a restricted sample of senate races, revealed that the press are more faithful to the messages presented by male candidates. This finding is reinforced when we look at press patterns for the full sample of U.S. Senate races. As the data in figure 4.5 indicate, the discussion of "male" issues in the news is much more prevalent than the discussion of "female" issues, following the male candidates' preferred agenda. However, "female" issues receive somewhat more attention for female candidates (40%) than for male candidates (30%). In addition, the presence of

FIGURE 4.5   *Percentage of "Male" and "Female" Issue Coverage in Senate Campaigns*

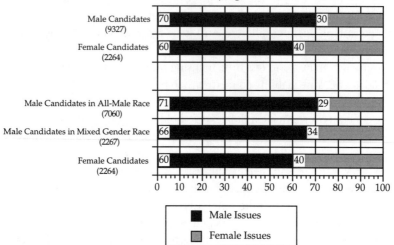

Note: "Male" issues include foreign policy, defense spending, arms control, foreign trade, farm issues, and the economy; "female" issues include day care, helping the poor, education, health care, women's rights, drug abuse, and the environment.

The difference in the issue coverage between male candidates and female candidates (overall) is statistically significant at $p < .01$. In addition, the difference in issue coverage between the male candidates in all-male races, the male candidates in mixed gender races, and the female candidates is statistically significant at $p < .01$. The p value is based on the difference in proportions test. The number in parentheses is the number of issue mentions coded for each type of candidate.

a woman in the race appears to change the agenda for male candidates. When men face female opponents, the press spend more time discussing "female" issues in their coverage of the male candidates.

While newspapers prefer to focus on "male" issues when covering men and women candidates for the U.S. Senate, women reporters are more likely to stress "female" issues in their coverage. Female reporters discuss issues such as education and health care 35 percent of the time while male reporters discuss these issues only about 28 percent of the time.[9] Moreover, when covering women candidates, female reporters devote 42 percent of their issue discussion to "female" issues, while male reporters spend only 19 percent of their time covering "female" issues.[10]

Women reporters may allocate greater space to the coverage of "female" issues because they believe these issues should be addressed by the candidates and considered by voters. In addition, the greater attention women reporters give to "female" issues, especially in their coverage of women candidates, also suggests that women reporters are more sensitive to the messages presented by women candidates. Women reporters, who may identify more closely with women candidates, respond by representing their campaign themes more faithfully. For these reasons, women reporters are an important resource for women candidates. Women candidates will be more successful in priming voters to think about their stereotypical strengths when female reporters are covering their campaigns. However, women reporters at major metropolitan papers are still relatively rare; only 24 percent of all the campaign articles in the newspaper sample were written by women.

Trait Coverage

Just as assessments of a candidate's viability and issue stands influence citizens' vote choice, so do judgments about a candidate's character (Abelson, Kinder, Peters, and Fiske 1982; Markus 1982). Voters use personality traits as a basis for evaluations of candidates in both national and statewide elections (e.g., Markus 1982; Goldenberg, Traugott, and Kahn 1988). The propensity to make trait-based evaluations of candidates may be related to the amount of trait information available to voters. If voters are provided with a great deal of information about a candidate's personality characteristics, then voters are likely to consider this information when developing impressions of candidates.

While men and women candidates mention their personal strengths in more than a third of their commercials (see chapter 3), reporters are reluctant to focus on the candidate's personality. Only about 15 percent of the news articles discuss the candidates' personal characteristics. In addition, reporters spend approximately the same amount of time describing the personal traits of men and women candidates for the U.S. Senate.

However, reporters use different terms to describe the personality traits of men and women candidates. Although women prefer to discuss "male" traits in their political communications, reporters are much more likely to refer to "female" traits such as compassion and honesty when describing women candidates compared to male candidates. In fact, as the data in table 4.1 indicate, 40 percent of all trait discussion in the news focuses on "female" traits for women candidates, while these "female" traits are mentioned half as often for male candidates. These data indicate that journalists are not following the candidates' lead when writing about the personal characteristics of women candidates. Instead, stereotypes appear to be influencing the coverage of these candidates.

Just as women candidates are described by reporters in stereotypically feminine ways, reporters emphasize stereotypically "male" traits when covering

TABLE 4.1
Percentage of "Male" and "Female" Trait Coverage in Senate Campaigns

Gender of Candidate	Male Traits[1]	Female Traits	N[2]	P-Value
Male Candidates	75	25	462	
				p<.01
Female Candidates	60	40	174	
Sex of Author	Male Traits	Female Traits	N	P Value
Male Author				
Male Candidates	64	36	383	
				n.s.
Female Candidates	63	37	72	
Female Author				
Male Candidates	81	19	59	
				p<.01
Female Candidates	52	48	46	

[1] "Male" traits include the following: independence, knowledge, objectivity, competitiveness, strong leadership, insensitivity, aggressiveness, lack of emotion, ambition, and toughness. "Female" traits include the following traits: dependence, noncompetitiveness, passivity, gentleness, strong emotions, weak leadership, and compassion.
[2] Entries are the number of male and female trait paragraphs, coded for each candidate type.

male candidates. For instance, reporters often refer to a male candidate's leadership ability or expertise when writing campaign stories. However, this emphasis on "male" traits echoes the male candidate's own preference for these traits, as illustrated by their advertisements.

As with issues, men and women reporters cover the traits of U.S. Senate candidates differently. However, women journalists are *less* responsive than male journalists to the trait emphasis of women candidates. Women reporters cover female candidates in a more stereotypical fashion than their male counterparts; they are more likely to emphasize "female" traits in their coverage of women candidates, even though the women candidates are trying to demonstrate their possession of stereotypically "male" traits.

Women reporters may stress "female" traits in their coverage of women candidates because they believe these are important personal characteristics that are undervalued in today's political arena. Or, women reporters may believe that talking about "female" traits will focus the public's attention on the women candidates' perceived strengths, thereby encouraging more positive impressions of women candidates. Whatever their intention, the fact remains that women reporters are less accurate than male reporters at representing the women candidates' preferred trait emphasis.

Voters see the political landscape largely through the eyes of the news media. In senate races, where direct contact with politicians is rare, citizens receive most of their news about the campaign from state newspapers. Voters' dependence on the press for political information may be problematic for women running for the U.S. Senate.

Women candidates running for the U.S. Senate do not receive the same press treatment as their male counterparts. Female candidates receive less news coverage and the coverage they do receive concentrates more on their viability and less on their issue positions. Furthermore, the press discussion of the candidates' viability is more negative for women candidates than for men, stressing the women's unlikely chances for victory as well as their lack of significant campaign resources. Given these gender differences in press treatment, voters' recognition of male candidates is likely to exceed that of female candidates, and evaluations of female candidates may be tied more closely to their perceived viability. Because female candidates are often considered noncompetitive by the press, the attention to the horse race could lead voters to develop more negative evaluations of female candidates. These results suggest that current patterns of press coverage may serve as a critical obstacle for women running for the U.S. Senate.

The gender of the reporter also influences how men and women are covered in the news. In particular, women reporters are more likely than their male colleagues to emphasize "female" issues and traits when covering women running for the U.S. Senate. Women candidates stress issues such as poverty, education, and child care in their campaigns, and female reporters are more likely than their male colleagues to echo this agenda in their coverage of senate campaigns.

With regard to traits, women candidates adopt a strategy of downplaying their stereotypical strengths. Women try to revise potentially damaging stereotypes by emphasizing their possession of typically "male" traits such as competence and experience. This strategy seems to be worthwhile since "male" traits are more highly valued by voters than "female" traits. As Huddy (1994) explains, "Based on evidence from research conducted over the last several decades, a female candidate stereotyped as a typical *feminine* woman would most certainly lose electoral support because she would be seen to lack typical male traits [thought to be] most necessary for effective national leadership." (Huddy 1994, p. 177).

While women candidates are trying to eradicate harmful stereotypes in their campaigns, women reporters are hindering these efforts by continuing to describe these candidates in stereotypically feminine ways. In fact, women reporters are less responsive than male reporters to the trait messages presented by women senate candidates. Women reporters may believe they are aiding women candidates by illustrating the importance of "female" traits in political campaigns, However, this strategy is likely to be unproductive since people believe that "male" traits are more important for elected officials.

Given that the news media differentiate between male and female candidates in their coverage of U.S. Senate campaigns, we need to assess whether these differences matter. In the next chapter I use an experimental design to examine the impact of gender differences in press coverage on people's impressions of men and women candidates for the U.S. Senate. By simulating current patterns of press coverage in the experiment, we can see whether gender differences in news attention lead people to develop more negative impressions of women candidates running for the U.S. Senate.

5

The Impact of Coverage Differences and Sex Stereotypes

❖

It is clear from the discussion in chapter 4 that the news media distinguish between male and female candidates in their coverage of Senate campaigns. Women candidates receive less coverage than their male counterparts, and the coverage they receive is more negative—emphasizing their unlikely chances of victory. These (and other) gender differences in news coverage may encourage voters to develop more positive impressions of male candidates than female candidates. Given the public's reliance on the news media for information about politics, gender differences in news coverage may influence the electability of women candidates for the U.S. Senate.

In this chapter I use an experiment to examine whether gender differences in news coverage influence people's views of male and female candidates. In the experiment I recreate the coverage patterns found in the content analysis and measure the influence these coverage differences have on people's impressions of senatorial candidates. With the experiment, we can see whether gender differences in news presentations influence people's views of male and female candidates.

Just as news reporters and editors distinguish between men and women candidates when covering senate campaigns, voters are likely to consider the gender of the candidate when forming impressions of candidates. With the present experimental design, by holding news coverage constant and giving people identical information about male and female candidates, we can see whether voters rely on sex stereotypes to draw distinctions between equivalent candidates. Finally, the experimental design allows us to examine the cumulative impact of both "gender" coverage and sex stereotyping on voters' evaluations of senate candidates.

Experimental Method

Development of Prototype Articles

Using the findings from the content analysis of news coverage as a guide, I created four newspaper articles which represented four distinct coverage patterns: male incumbent coverage, female incumbent coverage, male challenger coverage, female challenger coverage. A total of fourteen characteristics of coverage were used to create the four senate articles: four characteristics relate to the amount and prominence of coverage (e.g., length and location of article), six relate to general elements of campaign coverage (e.g., amount of horse race coverage, type of issue coverage), three relate to candidate characteristics and candidate resources (e.g., mention of candidate qualifications, discussion of campaign organization) and one indicates the gender of the author. Table 5.1 contains a complete listing of the coverage differences represented in the four senate articles.

These four prototype articles represent average differences in the coverage of male and female candidates in senate campaigns. The articles, by depicting the ways in which the news media differentiate between male and female candidates, simulate the type of articles that voters are likely to be exposed to during a campaign for the U.S. Senate. Since the results of the content analysis determine the ways in which the prototype articles vary, these articles represent composite differences in coverage. With these prototype articles, we can examine whether the aggregation of coverage differences influence people's perceptions of male and female senate candidates. The independent variable of interest, then, is not each individual coverage dimension (e.g., headline mention) but the composite differences (all fourteen dimensions) in coverage. These prototype articles, by illustrating how different types of candidates (e.g., male incumbents, female challengers) are typically covered during campaigns, allow us to examine the impact that gender differences in coverage have on people's views of senate candidates.

To illustrate how differences in news patterns are represented in the four senate articles, it is useful to present some examples. First, the results of the content analysis indicate that the press emphasize the horse race more when covering women senate candidates. In fact, almost one-third of the articles

TABLE 5.1
Summary of Differences in the Four Senate Articles

Coverage Characteristic	Male Incumbent Prototype Article	Female Incumbent Prototype Article
Length of Article	12 paragraphs	12 paragraphs
Paragraphs About Candidate	6 paragraphs	6 paragraphs
Prominence	Headline and Lead Mention	Lead Mention
Location	Page 12	Page 11
Issues	4 Paragraphs	3 Paragraphs
Content of Issues	"Male" Issues (economy, defense)	"Female" Issues (drugs, health)
Horse Race Coverage	1 Paragraph	3 Paragraphs
Horse Race Assessment	"Sure Winner"	"Competitive"
Criticism	1 Criticism	2 Criticisms
Positive and Negative Resources	No Mention	Mention of Positive and Negative Resources
Background	Mention	No Mention
Traits Mentioned in Article	"Insensitive"	"Effective"
Tone	Neutral	Mixture (Positive and Negative Tone)
Sex of Author	Male	Male

Coverage Characteristic	Male Challenger Prototype Article	Female Challenger Prototype Article
Length of Article	11 paragraphs	8 paragraphs
Paragraphs About Candidate	5 paragraphs	4 paragraphs
Prominence	No Headline or Lead Mention	Headline and Lead Mention
Location	Page 12	Page 18
Issues	3 Paragraphs	2 Paragraphs
Content of Issues	"Male" Issues (economy, defense)	"Male" Issues (economy)
Horse Race Coverage	1 Paragraph	2 Paragraphs
Horse Race Assessment	"Competitive"	"Somewhat less Competitive"
Criticism	No Mention	No Mention
Positive and Negative Resources	No Mention	Mention of Negative Resource
Background	No Mention	No Mention
Trait Mentioned in Article	"Strong Leader," "Dishonest"	No Trait Mentions
Tone	Neutral	Neutral
Sex of Author	Male	Female

written about women candidates mention the horse race while less than one-quarter of the articles written about male candidates discuss the horse race. Furthermore, this gender difference in coverage occurs for both incumbents and challengers. For instance, in most of the articles written about female incumbents, almost three paragraphs are devoted to the horse race while only about one paragraph discusses the horse race in articles about male incumbents. Similarly, most articles about female challengers contain about two horse race paragraphs while only one paragraph is devoted to the horse race in articles about male challengers. These modal differences are represented in the four senate articles, where one paragraph is devoted to the horse race in both the male incumbent article and the male challenger article while two paragraphs discuss the horse race in the female challenger article and three paragraphs are devoted to the horse race in the female incumbent article.

Along with gender differences in the quantity of horse race coverage, the content analysis revealed a systematic difference in the substance of the horse race discussion for men and women candidates. This disadvantage in viability assessments occurs for both female incumbents and female challengers. Male incumbents are usually described as "sure winners" while female incumbents are more likely to be considered "competitive." Among challengers, male candidates are most likely to be described by the press as "competitive" while female candidates are usually referred to as "somewhat competitive." Again, these modal differences are represented in the four prototype articles. In the male incumbent article, the candidate is described as a "sure winner" while the candidate in both the female incumbent article and in the male challenger article is described as "competitive." Finally, in the female challenger article, the candidate is described as "somewhat less competitive."

Design of Experiment

I conducted an experiment to see whether gender differences in news coverage and the sex of the candidate influence people's evaluations of male and female senatorial candidates. The experiment uses what is called a 2 X 4 factorial design with the manipulated variables being the sex of the candidate (male or female) and the type of news coverage (male incumbent coverage, female incumbent coverage, male challenger coverage, and female challenger coverage), represented by the four prototype articles.[1] For a description of the experimental conditions, see table 5.2.

TABLE 5.2
Description of Conditions in Senate Experiment

Condition	Senate Coverage Pattern		Sex of Candidate
1	Male Incumbent Coverage	+	Male Candidate
2	Male Incumbent Coverage	+	Female Candidate
3	Female Incumbent Coverage	+	Male Candidate
4	Female Incumbent Coverage	+	Female Candidate
5	Male Challenger Coverage	+	Male Candidate
6	Male Challenger Coverage	+	Female Candidate
7	Female Challenger Coverage	+	Male Candidate
8	Female Challenger Coverage	+	Female Candidate

I investigate three questions with this experimental design. First, do gender differences in news coverage influence individuals' evaluations of male and female candidates? By holding the sex of the candidate constant and only manipulating the type of press coverage, we can determine whether differences in news presentations influence people's perceptions of male and female candidates. Second, do people use gender as a cue when forming impressions of male and female senatorial candidates? By holding coverage constant and altering the sex of the candidate, we look at whether people rely on sex stereotypes to draw distinctions between identical male and female candidates. Third, do gender differences in news coverage *and* people's reliance on sex stereotypes influence people's evaluations of senate candidates? By allowing the type of coverage *and* the sex of the candidate to vary, we examine the cumulative impact that candidate coverage and the candidate's gender have on people's views of senatorial candidates.

As I discussed in Chapter 2, selected residents of the Ann Arbor/Ypsilanti community participated in the experiment, which lasted approximately one hour. Participants were randomly assigned to one of the experimental conditions, and in each condition participants read a newspaper page that included the prototype article about the senate candidates as well as two other articles about national politics. After reading the entire newspaper page, participants completed a questionnaire.[2]

Results

To assess whether the coverage differences depicted in the prototype articles influence people's views of the candidates, I looked at evaluations of the candidates along three dimensions. First, since people often consider a candidate's likelihood of election when casting their vote and since journalists distinguish between men and women in their coverage of the horse race, I examine people's assessments of the candidate's viability.

Second, since voters' impressions of a candidate's personal characteristics are likely to influence their overall view of a candidate, I measured people's evaluations of the candidate's personal traits. Prior research on voting behavior demonstrates that assessments of a candidate's honesty, leadership, and competence each affect people's overall evaluations of candidates. (Brady and Johnston 1987; Goldenberg, Traugott and Kahn 1988; Kinder and Abelson 1981; Markus 1982). For instance, if a voter is concerned about a candidate's competence, these concerns are likely to influence the voter's support for the candidate at the polls.

Third, people consider issues when developing impressions of senate candidates (e.g., Abramowitz and Segal 1986; Hinckley, Hofstetter, and Kessel 1974; Jacobson and Wolfinger 1989; Wright and Berkman 1986), and the salient issues in the campaign are likely to correspond to the issues receiving the most attention in the local press. Given the powerful role of the news media in affecting the public agenda, I look at people's assessments of the candidate's ability to deal with different policy areas.

The Influence of News Coverage on Candidate Evaluations

A series of two-way (coverage X gender) analyses of variance (ANOVAS) were conducted to assess the impact that coverage and gender have on evaluations of senate candidates. This analysis reveals that the four different prototype articles produce distinct candidate images. For instance, the four articles produce alternative assessments of the candidates' viability [$F(3,93)=10.6$, $p<.01$].[3] In fact, differences in coverage account for 42 percent of the variation in people's assessments of the candidates' viability.

Other evaluation differences are also influenced by the patterns of coverage. The prototype articles influence people's assessments of the candidates' ability to deal with defense issues, women's issue, and health issues.[4] Variations in coverage also influence assessments of the candidates' personality. Ratings of the candidates' leadership capabilities, honesty, and compassion all vary by coverage condition.[5]

To investigate the impact of coverage more thoroughly, we can look within status categories to see how people's impressions of candidates of the same status diverge when these candidates are covered differently in the

TABLE 5.3
The Impact of Coverage on Evaluations of the Senate Candidates

Question[1]	Male Incumbent Coverage[2] (Mean)	Female Incumbent Coverage (Mean)	T Value[3]	D.F.[4]
Leadership°	2.41	2.80	-2.04	45
Military°	3.14	3.67	-2.27	38
Viability°°	1.43	2.33	-4.97	52
Compassion°	2.67	2.04	2.58	46
Health°	3.45	2.67	3.42	44
Honesty°	2.74	2.22	2.48	44

	Male Challenger Coverage (Mean)	Female Challenger Coverage (Mean)	T Value	D.F.[4]
Viability°	2.50	2.91	-2.03	45

[1] See appendix 6 for exact question wordings.
[2] The smaller the number, the more positive the evaluation.
[3] One-tailed p values are presented for the issues explicitly mentioned in the coverage since coverage differences lead us to expect a directional difference in evaluations. Issues explicitly mentioned in the articles are viability assessments for all conditions and military assessments in the incumbent conditions. Two-tailed p values are presented for all other traits and issues.
[4] D.F. stands for degrees of freedom.
° p<.05
°° p<.01

news. The data in table 5.3 suggest that gender differences in news patterns are important and produce distinct images of the candidates—especially for incumbents. Candidates (male and female) receiving male incumbent coverage are considered likely to win their senate seats, while candidates (male and female) receiving female incumbent coverage are viewed as less viable. Similarly, candidates covered like a male incumbent are seen as stronger leaders than candidates who receive female incumbent coverage. Finally, the data in table 5.3 show that candidates receiving male incumbent coverage are viewed as significantly more competent at dealing with defense-related issues.

Gender differences in incumbent coverage, however, do not always advantage the candidate who is covered like a male incumbent. Participants view candidates receiving female incumbent coverage as more compassionate and more honest than candidates covered like male incumbents.[6] Candidates who are covered like female incumbents are also seen as better able to deal with health issues.

Coverage differences between male and female challengers are less influential, influencing only perceptions of the candidate's viability. The data in table 5.3 show that candidates who are covered like male challengers are seen as more electable than candidates who are covered like female challengers. Although the impact of gender differences in coverage is less extensive for challengers, differences in viability assessments are likely to be consequential.

The greater impact of incumbent coverage as compared to challenger coverage may be explained by the longer length of the incumbent articles. Since the content analysis of campaign coverage determined the length of the four senate articles, these experimental results suggest that news coverage of incumbents—because it is more extensive—is more consequential than news coverage of challengers.[7]

The incumbent articles may also be more powerful because participants rely on senatorial prototypes or schemas to process information about incumbents but not challengers. Psychological research suggests that prototypes (or schemas) help people process information more efficiently (e.g., Cantor and Mischel 1979), and the use of senatorial prototypes may make it easier for participants to digest information in the incumbent articles. Kinder, Peters, Abelson, and Fiske (1980) find that voters use presidential prototypes when evaluating incumbents but not presidential challengers, and the same process may be at work in the senate case. If participants are using senatorial prototypes to process incumbent information but not challenger information, then the information in the incumbent articles will be more influential since this information is interpreted more easily.

Finally, the incumbent articles may produce more striking differences in candidate images because the content of the two incumbent articles vary more profoundly than the content of the challenger articles. That is, there are dramatic differences in the coverage of men and women senators and it makes sense that the articles representing male and female incumbent coverage would produce divergent images of the candidates. Health issues, for instance, are discussed only in the female incumbent article, while economic issues are discussed in the three remaining senate articles. The greater content differences between the male and female incumbent articles—driven by actual gender differences in the coverage of sitting senators—help explain the greater coverage effects found in the incumbent conditions.

These results suggest that gender differences in coverage can be consequential but that these differences do not consistently advantage male candidates at the expense of female candidates. Candidates covered like male incumbents are advantaged along certain dimensions, while candidates who receive female incumbent coverage benefit in other ways. Coverage appears to be less influential for challengers, but candidates covered like male challengers are seen as more likely to win their electoral bids when compared to candidates covered like female challengers.

The Influence of Candidate Gender: Sex Stereotyping

Just as the news media distinguish between men and women candidates in their coverage, voters are likely to consider the gender of the candidate when forming impressions of senate candidates. The present experimental design, which allows us to see whether participants use sex stereotypes to draw distinctions between identical male and female candidates, illustrates the pervasiveness of stereotypes (see table 5.4). When participants are exposed to identical candidates, they view female candidates as better able to deal with education, health, and women's issues simply because they are women. For example, when participants are asked to rate the candidate's competence in dealing with the issue of women's rights, participants rate the female candidate as competent (2.3), while they rate the identical male candidate as somewhat incompetent (4.0). Participants also believe female candidates are more compassionate and more honest than their male counterparts.

TABLE 5.4
The Impact of Sex Stereotypes on Evaluations of the Senate Candidates

Question[1]	Male Candidate[2] (Mean)	Female Candidate (Mean)	T Value[3]	D.F.[4]
Compassion[*]	2.69	2.26	2.31	73
Education[**]	3.75	3.00	3.31	70
Health[**]	3.64	3.00	2.85	72
Honesty[**]	3.03	2.26	4.59	76
Honesty and Integrity[*]	3.42	2.91	2.48	85
Women[**]	4.00	2.30	7.47	70
Economy	3.32	3.22	0.45	81
Farm	3.34	3.37	-0.11	74
Knowledge	2.59	2.53	0.39	82
Leadership	2.81	2.73	0.46	76
Military	3.61	3.47	0.65	67

[1] See appendix 6 for exact question wordings.
[2] The smaller the number, the more positive the evaluation.
[3] Two-tailed p values are presented for all traits and issues.
[4] D.F. stands for degrees of freedom.
[*] p<.05
[**] p<.01

TABLE 5.5
The Impact of Sex Stereotypes on Evaluations of the Senate Candidates
(by Sex of the Respondent)

Question[1]	Male Candidates[2] (Mean)	Female Candidates (Mean)	T Value[3]	D.F.[4]
Male Respondents				
Honesty°°	3.09	2.40	2.04	29
Women°°	3.64	2.26	3.81	28
Compassion	2.38	2.33	0.20	29
Economy	3.31	3.35	-0.13	31
Education	3.27	3.00	0.65	28
Farm	3.40	3.56	-0.40	24
Honesty and Integrity	2.93	2.91	0.06	34
Knowledge	2.42	2.70	-1.12	30
Leadership	2.60	2.89	-1.06	27
Military	3.58	3.53	0.16	27
Female Respondents				
Compassion°	2.87	2.19	2.55	42
Education°°	4.00	3.00	3.51	40
Health°	3.73	3.04	2.34	42
Honesty°°	3.00	2.14	4.60	45
Honesty and Integrity°°	3.69	2.92	2.81	49
Women°°	4.19	2.33	6.03	40
Economy	3.32	3.12	0.74	48
Farm	3.32	3.23	0.29	48
Knowledge	2.67	2.40	1.53	50
Leadership	2.89	2.59	1.34	47
Military	3.62	3.42	0.77	38

[1] See appendix 6 for exact question wordings.
[2] The smaller the number, the more positive the evaluation.
[3] Two-tailed p values are presented for all traits and issues.
[4] D.F. stands for degrees of freedom.
° p<.05
°° p<.01

The data in table 5.4 also illustrate the pervasiveness of "female" stereotypes and the absolute absence of "male" stereotypes. For instance, female candidates are viewed as more honest and compassionate than identical male candidates but male candidates are not seen as stronger leaders or more knowledgeable than their female counterparts. Similarly, female candidates are considered more competent at dealing with "female" issues but male candidates are not viewed as more competent on "male" issues such as the economy, defense, and farm issues. These findings suggest that people do use stereotypes to distinguish between male and female candidates, yet these stereotypes always lead to more positive evaluations of women candidates.

Not all people are equally likely to use sex stereotypes when forming impressions of candidates. In particular, female respondents are much more willing to use gender as a cue to distinguish between male and female candidates. As the data in table 5.5 indicate, women respondents use stereotypes much more routinely than men. The reliance on these stereotypes encourages women to develop much more positive images of women candidates. Women respondents, for example, view women candidates as competent at handling educational issues (3.0), while they consider identical male candidates to be somewhat incompetent (4.0). Male respondents, on the other hand, do not consider women to be better equipped than men (3.0 v. 3.3) at dealing with these issues.

Women may stereotype more than men because the gender of the candidate may be especially salient to them. Female candidates are rare and their novelty could be more conspicuous to women voters. If this is the case, women respondents are likely to think about the gender of the candidate during the experiment and, therefore, to use stereotypes more frequently to draw distinctions between equivalent male and female candidates.[8] Similarly, women may be more likely than men to adopt certain feminist beliefs regarding the unique qualities that female candidates bring to office and may therefore use gender as a way of distinguishing between similar male and female candidates. Since women are more likely to employ stereotypes, women respondents develop more favorable views of female candidates.[9]

The Influence of Candidate Gender and Coverage

Given the independent impact of coverage effects and gender effects, it is important to examine the cumulative impact that news coverage differences *and* sex stereotypes have on people's perceptions of male and female candidates. I begin by looking at how (1) gender differences in coverage of male and female senators and (2) voters' stereotypical images of male and female senators affect people's views of candidates running for reelection. The data in table 5.6 show that coverage is more influential than gender for evaluations of incumbent candidates. Three of these coverage effects advantage the male incumbent, and two produce more positive evaluations of the female incumbent. Differences in coverage of male and female incumbents lead participants to believe that the male incumbent is more electable than his female counterpart, and participants believe that the male incumbent is a stronger leader and better able to deal with military issues. The gender dif-

TABLE 5.6
The Cumulative Impact of Candidate Gender and Candidate Coverage on Evaluations of the Senate Candidates

Question[1]	Male Incumbent Coverage with Male Candidate[2] (Mean)	Female Incumbent Coverage with Female Candidate (Mean)	T Value[3]	D.F.[4]
Coverage Effects				
Leadership[***]	2.50	3.08	-2.70	21
Military[**]	3.18	3.70	-1.86	19
Viability[***]	1.40	2.54	-4.40	24
Compassion[***]	2.83	1.77	3.19	23
Health[***]	3.73	2.54	4.03	22
Gender Effects				
Education[*]	3.45	2.92	1.88	22
Honesty[***]	3.08	2.00	4.93	23
Honesty and Integrity[*]	3.29	2.77	2.02	25
Women[***]	4.00	2.08	7.01	21

Question	Male Challenger Coverage with Male Candidate (Mean)	Female Challenger Coverage with Female Candidate (Mean)	T Value	D.F.
Coverage Effects				
Viability	2.71	3.00	-1.20	24
Gender Effects				
Education[***]	5.20	3.37	4.91	11
Health[***]	5.20	3.25	5.47	11
Honesty[***]	3.57	2.11	5.05	14
Women[***]	5.17	2.37	6.91	12

[1] See appendix 6 for exact question wordings.
[2] The smaller the number, the more positive the evaluation.
[3] One-tailed p values are presented for the issues explicitly mentioned in the coverage since coverage differences lead us to expect a directional difference in evaluations. Issues explicitly mentioned in the articles are viability assessments for all conditions and military assessments in the incumbent conditions. Two-tailed p values are presented for all other traits and issues.
[4] D.F. stands for degrees of freedom.
[*] p<.10
[**] p<.05
[***] p<.01

ferences in viability and leadership assessments are likely to be consequential since voters often consider the candidate's viability and leadership ability when developing overall impressions of the candidates. Similarly, given the importance of foreign policy issues in senate campaigns, (e.g., Kahn 1995; Tidmarch, Hyman, and Sorkin 1984), assessments of a candidate's competence for dealing with defense issues may influence people's overall impressions of senatorial incumbents.

Differences in coverage also lead participants to view the female incumbent as more compassionate and better able to deal with health issues. In terms of sex stereotypes, participants believe the female incumbent is more honest and can deal with education and women's issues more effectively than the male incumbent.[10] Unfortunately for women senators, these evaluation advantages are not likely to translate into an electoral advantage. First, since health, education, and women's issues rarely topped the senatorial agenda in the 1980s, assessments of the candidate's ability to deal with these issues were probably irrelevant. Put simply, voters were not likely to consider these issues when comparing competing candidates for the U.S. Senate. Second, traits such as honesty and compassion are largely inconsequential since voters view these traits as less important than leadership qualities for assessing electoral candidates (Huddy 1994).

Candidate coverage is much less influential for the challengers; differences in coverage of male and female challengers produce no differences in evaluations of the candidates. The difference in viability assessments found earlier (see table 5.3), is no longer statistically significant. By examining the viability ratings for candidates in the four challenger conditions (conditions 5–8)[11], we see why viability coverage is less powerful for the present comparison (condition 5 v. condition 7). This analysis shows that female candidates receive a bigger boost from the favorable viability content in the male challenger prototype article than their male colleagues.[12] The female challenger is considered more electable (2.20) when she receives male challenger coverage as compared to female challenger coverage (3.0). In comparison, people's views of the electability of the male challenger are less dependent on coverage differences, ranging from 2.71 when he is covered like a male challenger as compared to 2.82 when he receives female challenger coverage.

These results suggest that the content of horse race coverage is more influential for female challengers, with people's assessments of a female challenger's viability being more responsive to differences in press patterns. Perhaps because female challengers usually run in noncompetitive contests, information about a competitive woman candidate appears to stand out and is weighed more heavily by participants.

While gender differences in challenger coverage fail to influence evaluations, sex stereotypes are still powerful. Women challengers for the U.S. Senate are considered more honest than their male counterparts and they are also viewed as better able to deal with education, health, and women's issues. Yet, as with female senators, these particular advantages may not be particularly potent since these issues and traits were not salient in senatorial campaigns during the 1980s.

The Influence of Candidate Status

Finally, the status of the candidate is likely to influence people's perceptions of senate candidates. People may develop distinct impressions of incumbents and challengers and these differences in evaluations may be driven by differences in news patterns for challengers and incumbents. In addition, differences in impressions of incumbents and challengers may reflect the impact that status has on people's perceptions of candidates. Just as people have stereotypes about typical male and female candidates, people are likely to have stereotypical views of senators.

If voters have prototypical images of senators and they rely on these prototypes to judge competing candidates, then incumbency per se may act as an additional resource for senate incumbents. According to cognitive psychologists, people routinely use prototypes as cognitive shortcuts to make information-processing more efficient and allow people to fill in gaps in their information about other people. By linking together specific traits, issue expectations, and behaviors, these prototypes provide individuals with the ability to infer information about a wide range of attributes based on a small number of cues. (Rapoport, Metcalf, and Hartman 1989).

While previous work has not examined the substance of senatorial prototypes, some expectations can be offered. First, prototypical images of senators will be more positive than prototypical images of challengers. Senators, like presidents (Kinder, Peters, Abelson, and Fiske 1980), are likely to be viewed as strong leaders, inspiring, and knowledgeable. In addition, people will consider incumbents to be more knowledgeable about a variety of policy matters, since they have more experience than their challengers. If voters hold these types of prototypes, then the reliance on incumbency as a cue will lead voters to develop more positive images of incumbent candidates.

The role of incumbency in congressional elections has received a great deal of attention (e.g., Cover 1977; Ferejohn 1977; Fiorina 1977). Recent survey work suggests that voters are not attracted by incumbency per se but that incumbents are advantaged because they are more likely to be better known and better liked than their opponents (Jacobson 1987). In the present study, because each candidate is evaluated in isolation (the opponent of the candidate is never mentioned) and because the individual's information about the

TABLE 5.7
The Impact of Candidate Status on Evaluations of the Senate Candidates

Question[1]	Incumbent(Mean)[2]	Challenger(Mean)	T Value[3]	D.F.[4]
Health[**]	3.04	3.68	-2.77	72
Honesty and Integrity[*]	2.98	3.40	-1.98	85
Leadership[*]	2.62	3.00	-2.25	76
Viability[**]	1.83	2.70	-5.72	99
Vote[**]	2.64	3.16	-2.92	91

[1] See appendix 6 for exact question wordings.
[2] The smaller the number, the more positive the evaluation.
[3] Two-tailed p values are presented for all traits and issues.
[4] D.F. stands for degrees of freedom.
[*] p<.05
[**] p<.01

candidates is completely controlled, we can carefully examine the impact that candidate coverage and candidate status have on people's perceptions of incumbents and challengers. This experimental design, because of its control over people's political information, provides clues regarding the determinants of the incumbency advantage in senate elections.

In this analysis, by combining male and female candidates and comparing evaluations of challengers and incumbents, we can examine the impact that incumbency has on evaluations of the candidates. Although we cannot distinguish between coverage and status effects with this experimental design, we can see whether incumbents given incumbent coverage are evaluated differently from challengers who are given challenger coverage.

As the data displayed in table 5.7 indicate, participants consistently evaluate incumbents more positively than challengers. Some of these differences can be attributed to differences in the news coverage of incumbents and challengers. For instance, press coverage of the incumbent's viability, as represented in the senate articles, is more positive than the viability coverage associated with challengers. These differences in the news content encourage participants to view incumbents as more viable than challengers.

Other differences in participants' evaluations are not directly attributable to news coverage differences. For instance, participants give incumbents higher leadership ratings than challengers even though the leadership ability of the incumbents is not mentioned in their coverage. Leadership is discussed only in the male challenger prototype article, where the candidate stresses his (or her) leadership ability. Given these press patterns, the incumbency advantage in leadership assessments can not be due to coverage differences. Instead, this advantage is likely to be a pure status effect: incumbents are considered stronger leaders simply because they are U.S. senators. Finally, participants express a greater willingness to vote for incumbent candidates. This difference in vote intention is probably influenced both by content differences and by the status of the candidates.

These results show that people evaluate incumbents much more favorably than challengers. This advantage is primarily a function of different coverage patterns for incumbent and challengers. Yet, unlike past survey studies, these experimental results also suggest that the candidate's status influences evaluations. Incumbents are not advantaged simply because their opponents are less well-known and less popular. Instead, incumbency acts as a cue for voters, supplying them with additional information about the candidates. This added information favors the sitting senator, serving as an additional resource for the incumbent. The incumbency advantage found here—both in terms of status and coverage—will translate into a disadvantage for female candidates since female candidates run almost exclusively as challengers.[13]

The results of this experiment suggest that gender differences in news coverage hurt women senate candidates. Coverage differences are more dramatic for incumbents; these press patterns lead people to view male incumbents as stronger leaders, more viable, and better able to deal with defense issues. The press also differentiate between male and female challengers in their coverage of senate campaigns, and these differences lead people to view female challengers as less electable than their male counterparts.

While gender differences in news coverage often hurt women candidates, people's reliance on sex stereotypes leads them to develop more favorable impressions of women candidates. For instance, people consider women to be more competent than men at dealing with education and health policy. Women are also viewed as more compassionate and more honest than equivalent male candidates.

Given that sex stereotypes lead people to develop more favorable impressions of women candidates while news coverage patterns hinder women candidates, it is important to consider the relative importance of these two factors. Recent work in the field of electoral behavior suggests that certain evaluation dimensions are more important than others. Research suggests, for instance, that assessments of a candidate's competence and leadership are more influential than beliefs about a candidate's compassion (e.g., Kinder 1983; Markus

1982). Thus, because gender differences in coverage lead people to view male incumbents as strong leaders, these differences are more consequential than stereotypical beliefs about a woman candidate's compassion.

Similarly, not all issues will be equally prominent in campaigns for the U.S. Senate. In particular, issues that receive a great deal of press attention are more likely to be considered by voters appraising senatorial candidates. Consequently, "female" issues, which typically receive less coverage than "male" issues in senate campaigns, will be less salient to voters. Thus women's stereotypical advantages with regard to health, education, and women's issues are likely to be largely ineffectual during an actual campaign.

Finally, voters are likely to assess the candidates' viability when forming impressions of competing senate candidates. Although models of senate vote choice have not examined the impact of viability assessments, research at the presidential levels suggests that a candidate's viability is consequential, especially when voters have little information about the competing candidates. For example, Brady and Johnston's (1987) study of presidential primary voting suggests that a candidate's viability is more important than trait and issue stands for understanding voters' overall impressions of the candidates. This is a potential problem for women, since patterns of campaign coverage consistently lead people to view women senate candidates as less electable than their male counterparts.

In addition to being hindered by gender differences in news coverage, women are at a disadvantage in elections because they run primarily as challengers. The experimental findings demonstrate that both coverage and status differences lead people to view incumbents more positively than challengers. For instance, incumbents are considered stronger leaders and more viable than challengers.

Political Implications

Women candidates may want to consider these experimental results as they adopt campaign strategies in U.S. Senate races. A female incumbent who can manipulate the media's agenda because of her status as an incumbent may want to emphasize "female" issues in her campaign appeals. If a female incumbent can make "female" issues most salient to the voters, then she will gain an advantage in voters' evaluations. If voters believe that "female" issues are most important, then voters' sex stereotypes may lead them to develop positive evaluations of the female incumbent. The reliance on these primed dimensions, coupled with female stereotyping, will produce favorable evaluations of the female incumbent.

Although this strategy has short-term benefits, it also has long-term drawbacks in that such a strategy may perpetuate the female stereotype. For instance, voters will not be encouraged to revise their image of the compassionate female candidate who can deal more effectively with education and health issues than defense and economic issues. Consequently female challengers who cannot control the media's issue agenda will be evaluated by voters who (1) have stereotypical views of women candidates and (2) are concerned with the traditionally salient "male" issues that tend to dominate campaign coverage. This combination will lead to negative evaluations of the female challenger. Thus the female incumbent strategy of emphasizing female candidates' traditional strengths will sustain female stereotyping and therefore prove to be a disadvantage to the female challenger competing in a male-dominated arena. Given that more female challengers than incumbents seek election, this incumbent strategy is short-sighted; it does not help women increase their chances of holding high-level political office.

Instead, female incumbents may find it more prudent to emphasize their leadership ability and to demonstrate their competence in dealing with traditional "male" issues. Since incumbents receive such prominent coverage, female incumbents acting in a nonstereotypical fashion may encourage the modification of voter stereotypes. Recent research on the revision of stereotypes suggests that such a strategy may be successful (Weber and Crocker 1983). Using the candidacies of female incumbents to alter sex stereotypes may ease the way for more female candidates. If voter stereotypes can be eradicated, then voters will use the same criteria for judging male and female candidates and female senate candidates may find it easier to win elective office.

6

Differences in Campaign Appeals for Governor

✹

In the preceding chapters I have demonstrated that stereotypes affect the content and consequences of U.S. Senate campaigns. Senate candidates pursue strategies that are consistent with the public's prototypical images of men and women. In addition, the news media differentiate between male and female candidates in their coverage of U.S. Senate campaigns, and these differences lead people to develop more negative impressions of female candidates. These results suggest that women candidates face considerable constraints when running for the U.S. Senate.

While women candidates for the U.S. Senate face a daunting political environment, women candidates for governor are in a more enviable position. Unlike U.S. Senate races, where the salient issues of the campaign often highlight women candidates' perceived weaknesses, the relevant issues in gubernatorial campaigns tend to correspond to women's stereotypical strengths. A content analysis of state of the state addresses shows that gubernatorial agendas in the 1980s focused on child care and the environment as well as on policies related to key state services, such as education and health care (Herzik 1991). Each of these issue dimensions coincides with women's perceived areas of expertise.

Since the relevant policy domains vary according to the electoral office, the consequences of sex stereotypes also change with the electoral context. When the prominent issues of the campaign correspond to a woman candidate's perceived weaknesses, stereotypes held by voters will hinder women in their electoral bids. In contrast, when the important campaign themes complement a woman candidate's stereotypical strengths, then stereotypes are advantageous to women. The correspondence between the campaign context and stereotypical images held by the public will determine whether women will be helped or hurt by stereotypes.

Given that the impact of stereotypes is contingent upon the campaign setting, men and women candidates are likely to consider the prevailing electoral setting when choosing among political strategies. In particular, since certain stereotypical beliefs will be more powerful in senate campaigns, while others will be more consequential in gubernatorial races, candidates for these two offices will pursue different tactics. In this chapter I test the validity of this claim by examining the political commercials of candidates running for governor between 1982 and 1988 and comparing these messages to those presented by senate candidates.[1]

The Style of Advertisements in Gubernatorial Campaigns

As I discussed in chapter 3, men and women senate candidates develop political commercials that differ both in style and substance. For instance, women running for the U.S. Senate rely on "attack" advertisements significantly more often than their male counterparts. However, in gubernatorial elections, where women can highlight their stereotypical strengths in a political setting that places a premium on such strengths, women largely refrain from negative advertising. Instead, women gubernatorial candidates prefer to focus on their own candidacies and avoid attacking their opponents. Women candidates for governor use "attack" commercials 22 percent of the time, while women running for the U.S. Senate use such commercials twice as often (46%).[2]

As an illustration of these interoffice differences, Millicent Fenwick, in her bid for New Jersey's open senate seat in 1982, repeatedly attacked her opponent in a series of political commercials. Relying on an anonymous announcer, Fenwick questioned Frank Lautenberg's integrity and raised concerns about his qualifications to be a U.S. senator. In contrast, Madeline Kunin, running for an open gubernatorial seat in Vermont in 1988, opted for a more positive campaign appeal. She chose to emphasize her commitment to the environmental and the educational future of Vermont rather than repeatedly criticize her opponent.

FIGURE 6.1   *Percentage of Negative Commercials in Gubernatorial Campaigns*

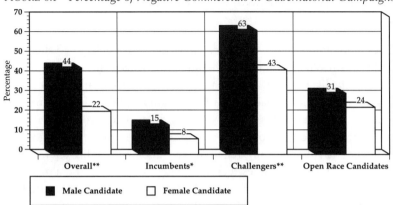

Note: Negative commercials are commercials that contain criticisms of the candidate's opponent. The numbers in the parentheses are the number of commercials examined for each type of candidate; the number of male candidates' commercials is followed by the number of female candidates' commercials. The p value is based on the difference in proportions test.
$p < .10$
$p < .05$

Women candidates for governor also employ negative advertisements less frequently than male gubernatorial candidates. As the data in figure 6.1 illustrate, women candidates for governor are less likely than male candidates to employ negative commercials, regardless of their status.[3] For example, male challengers for governor air negative advertisements almost two-thirds of the time, while women challengers attack their opponents in fewer than half of their commercials.

By largely rejecting "attack" politics, women gubernatorial candidates are probably pursuing a preferable strategy. As I have discussed earlier, negative campaigning is problematic for women candidates, since aggressive attacks violate norms about what is considered proper feminine behavior (e.g., Trent and Friedenberg 1983). Furthermore, considerable academic research suggests that negative advertising, in general, is counterproductive. "Attack" ads, although more memorable than positive advertisements (Ansolabehere, Behr, and Iyengar 1993; Basil, Schooler, Reeves 1991; Kern 1989; Lang 1992; Newhagen and Reeves 1989), often generate negative impressions of the candidate who is airing the advertisement.[4] This "boomerang" effect has been demonstrated by several researchers using different types of experimental designs (e.g., Basil, Schooler, Reeves 1991; Garramone 1984; Kahn and Geer 1994; Merritt 1987; Pfau and Burgoon 1988).[5]

The Discussion of Issues in Advertisements for Governor

The examination of senate campaign advertisements in chapter 3 shows that candidates stress policy in most of their commercials, with men and women about equally likely to talk about issues. When we turn to gubernatorial elections, we find a similar pattern. Gubernatorial candidates—both men and women—talk about their issue priorities in three-quarters of their commercials. However, the types of issues discussed in advertisements for governor and senator vary dramatically, reflecting the differences in the relevant issue domains for these two offices. Foreign policy issues consume almost one-quarter of all issue discussion in senate races, while these issues are completely absent in gubernatorial contests. On the other hand, gubernatorial candidates focus more attention on social programs than their colleagues in senate campaigns.

Since many of the prominent issues in gubernatorial campaigns highlight women's stereotypical strengths, women candidates have the flexibility to adopt one of two distinct strategies. On the one hand, women candidates can try to exploit people's stereotypes by focusing even more attention on women's perceived areas of expertise: health care, child welfare, education, the environment. On the other hand, since such perceived strengths are already prominent in gubernatorial races, women will have an advantage along these dimensions even if they spend little time emphasizing these issues in their campaigns. Instead, women candidates may take advantage of the favorable electoral climate and try to change potentially damaging stereotypes. In particular, women may want to dispel harmful preconceptions about their competence in dealing with fiscal matters.

Male candidates for governor face a different dilemma than their female counterparts. Men may highlight their stereotypical strengths by discussing economic issues in their gubernatorial advertisements or they can try to revise harmful perceptions of their candidacies by illustrating their competence in dealing with traditionally "female" issues. Unlike male senate candidates, male gubernatorial candidates have a greater incentive to pursue this second strategy, since "female" issues are likely to be considered by voters in gubernatorial elections.

According to the data in figure 6.2, gubernatorial candidates are more likely than senate candidates to try to eradicate stereotypes in their commercials by stressing their competence in areas where they are typically viewed as

FIGURE 6.2   *The Discussion of Issues in Senate and Gubernatorial Commercials*

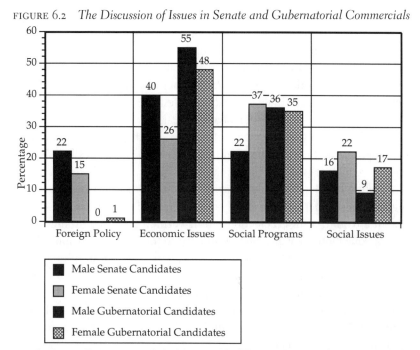

Note: The "foreign affairs" category includes discussion of the following: USSR-U.S. relations, arms control, Central America, South Africa, the Middle East, and Europe. The "economic issues" category includes discussion of the following: taxes, the federal budget, and discussion of the economy generally. The "social program" category includes the discussion of education, health programs, employment, welfare programs, and programs for the elderly. The "social issues" category includes the discussion of gay rights, abortion, school prayer, women's rights, civil rights, the environment, and drugs. For male senate candidates, the percentage of issue discussion was based on 324 issue mentions in the commercials; for female senate candidates, the percentage of issue discussion was based on 82 issue mentions in the commercials; for male gubernatorial candidates, the percentage of issue discussion was based on 212 issue mentions in the commercials; for female gubernatorial candidates, the percentage of issue discussion was based on 75 issue mentions in the commercials.

The following gender differences in emphasis are statistically significant: (1) discussion of foreign policy by male and female senate candidates (p < .10); (2) discussion of economic issues by male and female senate candidates (p < .01); (3) discussion of social programs by male and female senate candidates (p < .01); (4) discussion of social issues by male and female senate candidates (p < .10); and (5) discussion of social issues by male and female gubernatorial candidates (p < .10). The p value is based on the difference in proportions test.

weak. Women candidates for governor emphasize their competence at dealing with economic issues more often than women senate candidates.[6] Similarly, male gubernatorial candidates spend more time than male senate candidates documenting their commitment to social programs such as education and health care.[7]

Kay Orr, in her bid for the governorship of Nebraska in 1986, tried to reduce harmful stereotypes when she stressed economic issues in her victorious campaign. In several commercials, Orr illustrated her fiscal prowess and contrasted her economic plans with those of her opponent. Similarly, Governor George Deukmejian of California focused on male candidates' stereotypical weaknesses by illustrating his commitment to education. In one political commercial, Deukmejian explains, "As governor, I increased funding to the highest level in twenty years, put the basics back, and test scores are up again."

In addition to confronting stereotypical weaknesses in their commercials, male and female gubernatorial candidates also spend a significant amount of time emphasizing their stereotypical strengths. Male candidates for governor mention economic issues in more than half of their political advertisements (55%), while female gubernatorial candidates discuss social issues and social programs in 52 percent of their commercials. For example, Governor Madeline Kunin, in her reelection bid in Vermont, focused on the importance of education. "My own life is testimony to the power of learning. That's why I've fought so hard for money for education" says Kunin in one of her political advertisements. Democrat Bob Casey, in his 1986 bid for the governorship of Pennsylvania, stressed his perceived strengths when he pledged to improve his state's economy. In one of his commercials, Casey described his intention to "work with the best minds in the state to develop a comprehensive plan to revive [the] economy."

This dual emphasis on stereotypical strengths and weaknesses leads to only slight differences in the issue emphases of male and female candidates for governor. Overall, men and women gubernatorial candidates stress issues that differ only marginally. Senate candidates, in contrast, pursue their stereotypical strengths in their political commercials, thereby leading to sharp divisions in the policy priorities discussed by male and female candidates.

The Discussion of Traits in Advertisements for Governor

While the context of gubernatorial campaigns offers women candidates some important benefits, these candidates do not always have the advantage when compared with their senate colleagues. In particular, the office of governor presents some unique obstacles for women candidates. Unlike the position of U.S. senator, the position of governor involves managing the affairs of the state. Witt, Paget, and Matthews (1994) explain that "when voters see women candidates more as mothers than experienced politicians, they are unsure how a mother's compassion and empathy will play in the governor's chair." (Witt, Paget, and Matthews 1994: 116). To illustrate this point, the authors present California pollster Mervin Field's finding that during the 1990 gubernatorial election, voters were most concerned about whether Diane Feinstein was competent enough to handle the governorship. This hesitation persisted despite Feinstein's experience as an elected member of the San Francisco Board of Supervisors and her nine-year tenure as mayor of San Francisco.

Since people typically associate "male" traits such as aggressiveness, toughness, experience, and competence with their image of a desirable executive or manager (Huddy 1994; Witt, Paget, and Matthews 1994), women gubernatorial candidates who are perceived as lacking these traits may find that their campaigns are seriously handicapped. As Republican campaign consultant John Deardourff observed, "Men are perceived competent until proven otherwise, whereas women have to prove that they are competent (Witt, Paget, and Matthews 1994: 116).

To counter these stereotypical beliefs about their personal characteristics, women gubernatorial candidates focus on their personal traits much more often than any other type of candidate (i.e., male candidates for governor, male and female senate candidates). Women gubernatorial candidates mention their personal traits in almost two-thirds (64%) of their advertisements, while women senate candidates and male candidates for both governor and senator stress their personal traits in fewer than half of their commercials (41% for female senate candidates, 40% for male senate candidates, 44% for male gubernatorial candidates).[8] In fact, nonincumbent women running for governor, who are likely to be at more of a disadvantage along "male" trait dimensions than incumbent women governors, stress their personal strengths in about three-quarters of their advertisements (71% for female gubernatorial challengers, 76% for female candidates in open gubernatorial contests). Male nonincumbents in gubernatorial races, on the other hand, focus on personal traits in fewer than half of their ads (44% for male challengers, 47% for male candidates in open races).[9]

Furthermore, when describing their personal strengths, women candidates for governor stress their possession of "male" traits such as experience, leadership, and toughness almost exclusively. These women candidates mention "male" traits five times as often as "female" traits such as compassion and integrity. As the data in figure 6.3 indicate, women gubernatorial candidates highlight "male" traits much more frequently than male candidates. Women candidates describe themselves with these "male" adjectives 84 percent of the

FIGURE 6.3   *Gender Differences in the Discussion of "Male" and "Female" Traits*
in the Political Commercials of Gubernatorial Candidates

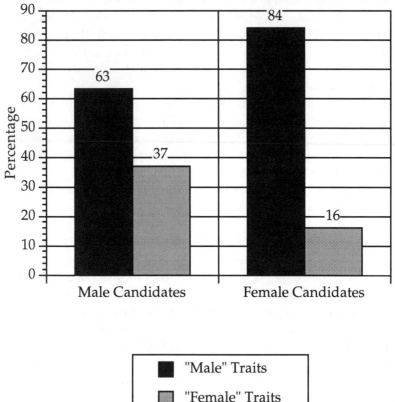

Note: "Male" traits include the following: independence, knowledge, objectivity, strong leadership, toughness; "female" traits include honesty, sensitivity, gentleness, and compassion. The difference in the discussion of "male" traits (and "female" traits) for male and female gubernatorial candidates is statistically significant at $p < .01$. The p value is based on the difference in proportions test. For male candidates, the percentages are based on 129 trait mentions in their commercials; for female candidates, the percentages are based on 80 trait mentions in their commercials.

time, while male candidates split their emphases on "male" and "female" traits more evenly, discussing "male" traits only 63 percent of the time.

Kay Orr's campaign exemplifies the female gubernatorial candidate's preference for highlighting "male" traits. She aired advertisements explicitly citing her experience with and competence in handling monetary issues, as documented by her tenure as state treasurer. Norma Paulus pursued a similar tactic in her bid for governor of Oregon in 1986. In contrast, Ned McWherter, a candidate for governor of Tennessee, aired commercials illustrating his "female" traits: in one advertisement, McWherter plays with a group of school children while a voice describes him as compassionate and honest.

News Coverage of the Candidates' Political Messages

Men and women candidates clearly adopt alternative strategies in the quest for the governorship. Women gubernatorial candidates, in contrast to their male counterparts, rely more heavily on positive appeals, focus more extensively on personal characteristics in their advertisements, and prefer to use "male" traits to describe themselves. Men and women rely on these divergent approaches because they believe that these messages will convince voters to support their candidacies. However, since voters understand that advertisements are aimed at changing their preferences, voters are not always influenced by these messages. News reports, on the other hand, are likely to be more influential, since people regard the news as more objective than campaign advertisements (Graber 1992). News reports are also more powerful because more people receive campaign information from the press than from political advertisements (Joslyn 1983). Given the power of the news media, campaign messages are likely to be more effective if the news media reinforce those messages.

As I described in chapter 3, the political messages of women senate candidates are largely ignored by the press, while the campaign rhetoric of male candidates is reproduced more faithfully in the media's coverage of male senate candidates' campaigns. In gubernatorial elections, we expect women candidates to be more effective than female senate candidates at garnering attention for their campaign themes. First, women candidates for governor, when compared with their counterparts in senate races, have been about three times as successful at winning statewide election (Center for the American Woman and Politics 1993). Therefore reporters are likely to take women gubernatorial candidates more seriously and, subsequently, pay closer attention to their campaign themes. In addition, women gubernatorial candidates spend more time than women senate candidates talking about traditionally salient issues, such as the economy. These types of issues are likely to catch the attention of reporters more easily than the discussion of nonconventional issues.

With regard to news coverage of issues, the data in table 6.1 show that the press continue to represent the messages of male candidates more faithfully

TABLE 6.1

Comparison of Spot Ads and News Coverage in Gubernatorial Campaigns[1]

| | Issues | | | |
| | Male Candidates | | Female Candidates | |
	News Coverage	Spot Ads	News Coverage	Spot Ads
"Male" Issues[2]	53%[a]	55%[b]	60%[ac]	68%[bc]
"Female" Issues	47%	45%	40%	32%
	(5115;21)[3]	(183;21)	(1710;7)	(77;7)

| | Traits | | | |
| | Male Candidates | | Female Candidates | |
	News Coverage	Spot Ads	News Coverage	Spot Ads
"Male" Traits[4]	66%	68%[d]	66%[e]	81%[de]
"Female" Traits	34%	32%	34%	19%
	(1090;21)[5]	(129;21)	(196;7)	(80;7)

[1] Cells sharing superscripts are significantly different from each other. The p value is based on the difference in proportions test.
[2] "Male" issues include foreign policy, defense spending, arms control, foreign trade, farm issues, and the economy; "female" issues include day care, helping the poor, education, health care, women's rights, drug abuse, and the environment.
[3] Entries are the number of "male" and "female" issue mentions, coded for each candidate type, followed by the number of candidates.
[4] "Male" traits include the following: independence, knowledge, objectivity, strong leadership, and toughness; "female" traits include honesty, sensitivity, gentleness, and compassion.
[5] Entries are the number of "male" and "female" trait mentions, coded for each candidate type, followed by the number of candidates.
[a,e] $p \leq .01$
[b,d] $p \leq .05$
[c] $p \leq .10$

than they represent those of women candidates.[10] While the degree of incongruity between the media's emphasis and women gubernatorial candidates' messages is somewhat smaller here than in races for U.S. senator, the media continue to echo the rhetoric of male gubernatorial candidates more accurately. Specifically, the difference between news coverage and the gubernatorial candidates' messages is 2 percent for male candidates and 8 percent for women candidates.

The news media's greater responsiveness to male candidates is even more impressive when we look within status categories. Male governors, for example, mention "male" issues in 53 percent of their advertisements, and the news media reflect this emphasis by discussing "male" issues 54 percent of the time. Female governors, on the other hand, focus on "male" issues 63 percent of the time. The media do not reflect this emphasis, however; they mention "male" issues in only half of their coverage of women incumbents. Similarly, female candidates in open races for governor focus on "male" issues almost twice as often as their male counterparts (79% v. 49%). However, the news coverage given to these two types of candidates is barely distinguishable. Forty-three percent of the coverage of female candidates focuses on "male" issues, while 46 percent of the coverage of male candidates discusses these issues.

When men and women candidates for governor discuss their personal characteristics in their advertisements, they use different traits to describe their personalities. In particular, women are more likely to emphasize their competence and experience in their campaign communications. Yet, consistent with findings presented earlier, the news media do not represent the female candidates' emphases. The correspondence between what the candidates say and what the news media report is nearly identical for male candidates (2% difference between news coverage and spot ads). However, the correspondence is significantly weaker for women candidates (15% difference between news coverage and spot ads).

As with issues, this gender difference in media correspondence is not a reflection of status differences between men and women gubernatorial candidates. For example, among candidates running for open gubernatorial seats, men talk about "male" traits in 62 percent of their advertisements and the news media cover these same traits 62 percent of the time. On the other hand, female candidates in open races stress "male" traits in almost nine out of ten ads (86%), yet "male" traits are discussed only about half of the time (57%) in media coverage of their campaigns.

These results demonstrate that the correspondence between the news media's coverage and the candidates' campaign themes is higher for male candidates, regardless of the electoral arena (e.g., senator or governor), the topic of coverage (e.g., issues or traits), and the status of the candidates (e.g., incumbents, challenger, open race candidates). In gubernatorial campaigns, women often campaign by emphasizing their ability to deal with "male" issues and by illustrating their possession of "male" traits. However, the news media's unresponsiveness to these messages—especially with regard to the coverage of their personal characteristics—blunts the effectiveness of women candidates' campaign strategies. This lack of congruity between women candidates' rhetoric and press coverage of the campaign represents an important obstacle for women candidates.

This analysis of the political advertisements of twenty-eight gubernatorial candidates shows that men and women campaign differently for the office of governor. Women candidates are less likely than men to engage in "attack" advertising, are more likely to dress professionally in their commercials, and spend much more time illustrating their experience, competence, and strength.

In addition, the comparison of senate and gubernatorial advertisements shows that the campaign setting influences the strategies adopted by male and female candidates. For example, women gubernatorial candidates, in contrast to their colleagues in races for U.S. senator, compete for votes in a more favorable setting, which leads women gubernatorial candidates to employ positive advertisements more frequently than women senate candidates.

Similarly, differences in the electoral context influence the types of issues pursued by candidates. In gubernatorial campaigns, where "female" issues are more salient, male candidates try to reduce potentially damaging stereotypes by stressing "female" issues more often than their counterparts in senate races. Women candidates for governor also try to revise stereotypes in their campaign appeals. For example, they are more likely than female senate candidates to illustrate their ability to deal with such "male" issues as the economy.

When choosing a particular campaign appeal, candidates weigh the potential electoral benefits of alternative strategies. For example, women gubernatorial candidates spend a great deal of time demonstrating their possession of "male" traits in an effort to secure support for their candidacies. Male gubernatorial candidates, on the other hand, do not feel compelled to focus exclusively on "male" traits in their political messages.

Men and women choose specific appeals because they believe that such strategies will be effective in garnering votes. However, the news media are not very receptive to the messages presented by women candidates, thereby reducing the potency of the women candidates' advertising strategies. In both senate and gubernatorial elections, the news media often distort the campaign themes of women candidates, while they accurately represent the messages of male candidates. These gender differences in news coverage are likely to hinder women as they seek the offices of governor and U.S. senator.

In the next chapter I continue with a more extensive analysis of news coverage in gubernatorial campaigns. Complementing the earlier examination of senate races, I look at how the context of the campaign affects media coverage of men and women gubernatorial candidates and how these coverage patterns, along with people's stereotypes, influence people's perceptions of these candidates.

7

Press Coverage of Male and Female Candidates for Governor

✵

In this chapter I examine how changes in the campaign context influence press coverage of women candidates for governor. Compared with their colleagues in senate races, women gubernatorial candidates are likely to receive more favorable news treatment for a number of reasons. First, as I have discussed earlier, the correspondence between the salient issues in gubernatorial contests and women's stereotypical strengths could produce more positive coverage. Second, historical differences in the electability of women candidates can influence coverage patterns in senate and gubernatorial races. Because women have been more successful in winning election to governor than senator, the press are likely to take women gubernatorial candidates more seriously and focus less intensely and less negatively on their electability.

In addition, differences in the electoral characteristics of the two offices could encourage more equitable press treatment of women gubernatorial candidates. In particular, incumbency plays a less powerful role in gubernatorial races than senate races (Piereson 1977; Seroka 1980; Wright 1974). Incumbent governors, for example, have significantly lower success rates than senators (Seroka 1980), and incumbent governors are not viewed as favorably as their senatorial counterparts (Wright 1974). Since the incumbency advantage is less daunting in gubernatorial campaigns, women running as challengers can expect more even-handed coverage than their less fortunate colleagues in U.S. Senate races.

Relatedly, differences in the general patterns of news coverage in senate and gubernatorial campaigns can advantage women candidates for governor. In particular, press coverage for all candidates is more equitable in gubernatorial races—regardless of status or the competitiveness of the race—with all types of candidates receiving approximately the same amount of news coverage (Kahn 1995). In contrast, noncompetitive candidates and challengers in senate races receive significantly less press attention than incumbents and competitive candidates (Kahn 1991). Since all candidates receive a fair amount of press attention in gubernatorial races, women candidates (who often run as nonincumbents) are likely to garner more press attention than women running for the U.S. Senate.

Quantity of Campaign Coverage

As I have discussed in chapter 4, women senate candidates consistently receive less coverage than their male counterparts. Even when one controls for the competitiveness of the senate contest and the size of the state newspaper, journalists devote less news space to the coverage of women's campaigns for the U.S. Senate. Gender differences in the amount of press coverage in gubernatorial races are less dramatic.[1] While races with male gubernatorial candidates receive slightly more coverage than those with female candidates, these differences are neither statistically significant nor substantively important. Furthermore, since women gubernatorial candidates are more likely than men to run in states with small newspapers, the differences in the amount of coverage may merely reflect the difference in sizes of the state newspapers. In races that include women candidates, the average size of the state newspaper is 3,750 column inches, while newspapers in all-male races average about 4,548 column inches.[2]

In addition, as the data in figure 7.1 show, the gender differences in news coverage are not consistent. Among competitive contests all-male races receive slightly more coverage than races that include female candidates; yet, among noncompetitive contests, races that include female candidates receive somewhat more coverage. Overall, the news media do not always neglect women candidates in their coverage of gubernatorial campaigns.

The coverage of individual candidates in gubernatorial contests, like the coverage of races, does not consistently advantage male candidates. On average, about seventy articles are written about male and female candidates during a gubernatorial campaign. For example, in the 1986 race for governor in Oregon, the *Portland Oregonian* published seventy-five articles about Neil Goldschmidt in his victorious campaign, while seventy-five articles were written about his opponent, Norma Paulus. Similarly, about sixteen paragraphs

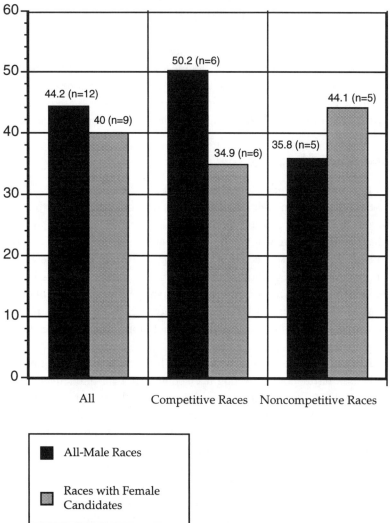

FIGURE 7.1 *Average Number of Paragraphs Published Each Day in Gubernatorial Races*

Note: None of the gender differences in the amount of coverage is statistically significant at the p < .10 level. The p value is based on the t statistic. The number in parentheses is the number of races examined for each category.

are published about male and female gubernatorial candidates in the local newspapers each day.

These results suggest that women candidates for governor, unlike their counterparts in senate campaigns, do not invariably receive less press coverage than their male counterparts. Since the press do not always allocate less coverage to the campaigns of women gubernatorial candidates, these candidates are likely to be more widely known than women running for U.S. senator.

Horse Race Coverage

Not only do women candidates for the U.S. Senate receive less coverage than male candidates, but in addition, the press focus more intensely on their viability and the substance of this discussion is primarily negative. In gubernatorial campaigns, where women are more likely to run competitive and successful campaigns, horse race coverage is not as pervasive. Fifteen percent of all campaign stories, regardless of the candidates' gender, are devoted to the horse race. Whether they are competing in competitive or noncompetitive races or as incumbents, challengers, or candidates in open races, women gubernatorial candidates receive about as much horse race coverage as their male counterparts.[3]

In addition, when journalists do focus on the horse race, they do not consistently draw distinctions between the electability of male and female gubernatorial candidates (see figure 7.2). Unlike their colleagues in senate races, both male and female candidates are described as competitive by reporters.[4] In particular, women incumbents and challengers in gubernatorial contests are considered as electable as their male counterparts. For example, when Julie Belaga of Connecticut challenged Governor William O'Neill in the 1986 election, the press described Belaga as somewhat competitive (2.5). That same year, reporters described Tom Bradley's challenge of Governor George Deukmejian in similar terms (2.6) when covering the California race in the *Los Angeles Times*.

However, gender differences in horse race coverage are not completely absent in gubernatorial contests. Women candidates competing in open races are viewed as less electable than their male counterparts. While women candidates in these races are described as somewhat competitive (2.4), their male counterparts are often classified as competitive (2.9). Since women candidates often compete for open gubernatorial seats, these gender differences in viability assessments may prove to be an important obstacle for women. For

FIGURE 7.2   *Press Assessments Regarding the Viability of Gubernatorial Candidates*

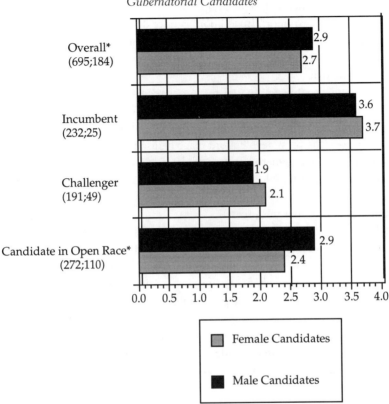

Note: Press viability assessments were rated on a four-point scale where 4 denotes "likely winner," 3 denotes "competitive," 2 denotes "somewhat competitive," and 1 denotes "sure loser." * indicates that the difference in press assessments is statistically significant at p < .01. The p value is based on the t statistic. The number in parentheses is the number of horse race paragraphs examined for each type of candidate; the number of paragraphs for male candidates is followed by the number of paragraphs for female candidates.

instance, between 1983 and 1988, 44 percent of all women running for governor were competing for open seats.

In addition to reporting on the horse race in their campaign coverage, journalists often focus on candidates' campaign resources. In senate campaigns reporters focus on negative campaign assets (e.g., lack of endorsements, lack of funding) much more frequently for women than for male candidates. Over one-tenth of all articles about women senate candidates mention negative resources, while only 5 percent of all the articles written about male candidates mention the candidate's lack of resources.

In gubernatorial races the discussion of negative resources is not as common with only 4 percent of all campaign articles mentioning the candidate's lack of campaign support. In addition, gender differences in coverage are far from substantial: 3 percent of all articles about male gubernatorial candidates focus on negative resources, compared with 5 percent of news stories about female candidates.

Although negative campaign resources receive little media attention in gubernatorial campaigns, discussion of the candidate's positive campaign assets, such as endorsements and fundraising abilities, is more common. Furthermore, the press devote more space to discussing the positive campaign resources of female gubernatorial candidates.[5] Overall, 15 percent of the articles written about female gubernatorial candidates mention their access to positive resources, while less than 10 percent of the articles about male candidates mention similar resources.[6]

To summarize, the press do not consistently distinguish between male and female gubernatorial candidates when discussing their probability of election. These coverage patterns deviate sharply from the patterns in senate races. Unlike citizens reading about senatorial campaigns, citizens relying on newspapers for information about gubernatorial campaigns are not likely to develop negative impressions of the electability of women gubernatorial candidates. In fact, with the significant amount of attention given to female candidates' campaign resources, readers could consider women candidates to be likely victors in their bids for the governor's chair.

Issues

While women candidates for governor do not face all the disadvantages endured by their counterparts in senate contests, gender differences in press treatment are not completely absent in gubernatorial campaigns. As in senate races, the press often pay less attention to the issue concerns of women candidates for governor. Overall, an average of 5.5 paragraphs a day are published about the issue priorities of male candidates, while only about 4.7 issue paragraphs are published about female candidates each day.[7]

Gender differences in issue coverage are most dramatic for challengers and candidates in noncompetitive races. Male challengers receive three times as much issue coverage as female challengers: six paragraphs a day are published about issues for male challengers and only two paragraphs a day discuss the issue concerns of female challengers.[8] Similarly, in noncompetitive races, almost half

(46%) of all the articles written about male candidates mention issues, while less than one-third (32%) of the articles about women candidates focus on policy matters.[9] As an illustration of these gender differences, consider the following example: when Chris Spirou challenged Governor John H. Sununu of New Hampshire in 1984, 6.1 paragraphs a day were written about Spirou's issue priorities in the *Manchester Union Leader*. In contrast, in 1986, when Patty Cafferta ran against Governor Richard H. Bryan of Nevada, she received on average only 1.7 issue paragraphs in the *Las Vegas Review Journal* each day.

The limited amount of attention devoted to issues for women in senate and gubernatorial races can hurt women's chances of election. Since less information is presented about the issue priorities of women candidates, voters are likely to be uncertain about whether these candidates can handle the pressing issues of the day, leading voters to withhold their support for these candidates at the polls. Why women receive less issue coverage than men is not clear. As I have discussed earlier, it could be that journalists are preoccupied with other themes when following women's campaigns (e.g., horse race for senate candidates) and, subsequently, less news space is available for coverage of the candidates' policy positions. Or, newspeople may believe that women are less competent than men at handling important issues, so women's views on issues are considered less important and less newsworthy. However, coverage of women's issue concerns is not a reflection of the candidate's own emphasis. The candidates' political advertisements demonstrate that women senate candidates and women gubernatorial candidates discuss their issue priorities just as frequently as their male colleagues.

In addition to devoting less attention to the issue positions of female gubernatorial candidates, reporters are less responsive to the issue agendas articulated by female candidates for governor. Women gubernatorial candidates prefer to discuss "male" issues, describing their commitment to these policy areas in more than two-thirds of their advertisements. However, the news media do not match their preference for "male" issues. Male candidates, in contrast, divide their attention almost equally between "male" and "female" issues in their commercials, and news coverage of these candidates accurately reflects this emphasis. These findings, first described in chapter 6, are reinforced when we examine press patterns for the full sample of gubernatorial races.[10] As the data in table 7.1 indicate, reporters, echoing the emphasis of male candidates, devote about the same amount of time to "male" and "female" issues in their coverage, showing only a slight preference for "male" issues when following the campaigns of women candidates.

TABLE 7.1

Percentage of "Male" and "Female" Issue Coverage in Gubernatorial Campaigns[1]

Gender of Candidate	Male Issues[2]	Female Issues	N[3]
Male Candidates	47[a]	53	8010
Female Candidates	55[a]	45	2124
Sex of Author	Male Issues	Female Issues	N
Male Reporter			
Male Candidates	48[b]	52	5391
Female Candidates	56[bc]	44	1243
Female Reporter			
Male Candidates	44	56	1259
Female Candidates	43[c]	57	310

[1] Cells sharing superscripts are significantly different from each other. The p value is based on the difference in proportions test.
[2] "Male" issues include foreign policy, defense spending, arms control, foreign trade, farm issues, and the economy; "female" issues include day care, helping the poor, education, health care, women's rights, drug abuse, and the environment.
[3] Entries are the number of male and female issue paragraphs for each candidate type.
[a,c] p<.01
[b] p<.05

This analysis also shows that women reporters do a poor job in reflecting the campaign agendas of women candidates for governor. Although women gubernatorial candidates spend significantly less time than male candidates discussing "female" issues, women reporters focus on "female" issues in the majority of their coverage, regardless of the candidate's gender. Male reporters, in contrast, discuss "female" issues somewhat less frequently when covering women gubernatorial candidates, reflecting the women candidates' preferred agenda.

Finally, by comparing press coverage of issues in senate and gubernatorial races, we can draw some conclusions about these campaigns. First, citizens reading about these two statewide contests are receiving information about different types of issues. In races for governor, issues such as education, child care, and the environment garner about half of all issue coverage (51%), while these same topics are discussed only about a third of the time in races for U.S. senator (29%).[11] These data substantiate the contention that the agenda in gubernatorial races highlight women's stereotypical strengths much more strongly than the press agenda in U.S. Senate races.

Second, gender differences in issue coverage are substantially smaller in gubernatorial races than senate races. This interoffice difference reflects the greater similarity in the messages delivered by male and female candidates for governor. While male and female candidates for U.S. senator spend most of their time stressing their stereotypical strengths, leading to striking gender differences in the candidates' themes, candidates for governor also try to alter stereotypes by emphasizing their stereotypical weaknesses (i.e., male gubernatorial candidates demonstrate their ability to deal with educational issues). This dual strategy of focusing on stereotypical strengths and weaknesses leads to greater overlap in the agendas of male and female gubernatorial candidates, producing similarities in the press coverage of their campaigns.

Third, these results indicate that women reporters favor "female" issues when following candidates for governor and senator, irrespective of the candidate's own emphasis. Women reporters may allocate more space to these issues because they feel these are important issues, which are often neglected in coverage of electoral campaigns. In senate races, this predilection for "female" issues corresponds with the emphasis of female candidates, leading to similarities between the women candidates' messages and coverage by women reporters. In gubernatorial contests, in contrast, women candidates choose to highlight "male" issues, leading to a great disparity between the women candidates' agenda and reporting patterns by women journalists.

Personality Traits

In addition to viability assessments and issue evaluations, perceptions of a candidate's personality characteristics influence people's overall evaluations of political candidates. While traits are most important in presidential contests where information about the candidates is plentiful, these types of evaluations are often consequential in statewide campaigns (Goldenberg, Traugott, and Kahn 1987). Overall, traits receive significantly more press attention in gubernatorial races than in senate races, which suggests that voters' impressions of each candidate's personality may play a more central role in gubernatorial contests (Kahn 1995).

Among gubernatorial candidates, the attention to traits is more extensive for women candidates. As the data in figure 7.3 illustrate, women consistently receive more trait coverage than their male counterparts. This gender difference in trait emphasis is remarkably consistent and occurs for all types of candidates. For example, almost one-quarter (23%) of all articles written about women in competitive campaigns mentioned traits, while only one-sixth (17%) of the articles about male competitive candidates touched on the candidate's personal characteristics.

The greater press attention given to the personal attributes of women candidates reflects the candidates' own campaign themes; women describe their

FIGURE 7.3   *Percentage of Articles Mentioning Traits in Gubernatorial Races*

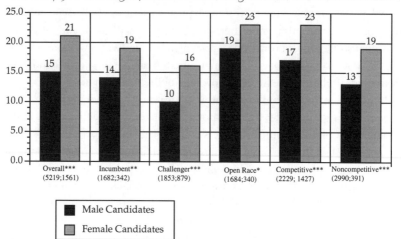

Note: The numbers in parentheses are the number of articles about male candidates followed by the number of articles about female candidates. The p value is based on the difference in proportions test.
*** p < .01
** p < .05
* p < .10

personality characteristics more often than men in their political communications (see chapter 6). While the press are receptive to gender differences in the candidates' emphasis on traits, this responsiveness has been absent in other content areas. For example, reporters allocate less space to the issue preferences of women candidates, even though women talk about issues as often as their male counterparts.

Reporters follow the lead of women candidates by stressing traits more frequently when following their campaigns. However, reporters and women candidates are not focusing on the same types of traits. Women try to dispel damaging preconceptions about their leadership ability, experience, and competence by focusing on "male" traits almost exclusively in their ads. Reporters, in contrast, use these terms significantly less often when describing women candidates. Women rely on "male" adjectives over 80 percent of the time in their campaign commercials, while journalists use these terms only 66 percent of the time.[12] Furthermore, male and female reporters are equally likely to misrepresent the messages of women candidates: both men and women reporters focus on "male" traits two-thirds of the time when following women's campaigns.

Male candidates do not battle negative impressions of their competence; consequently, they are less likely than women to stress "male" traits in their commercials. The press perfectly mirror the campaign messages of male candidates; male candidates and journalists covering their campaigns focus on "male" traits 65 percent of the time. A preponderance of trait information is available about women gubernatorial candidates, encouraging voters to consider the candidates' personality characteristics when casting their vote. The substance of trait coverage may disadvantage women candidates however, since journalists—both men and women—spend less time than women candidates would like documenting the candidates' possession of "male" traits. Given these coverage patterns, people's stereotypical images of women candidates are likely to persist, leading to negative impressions of women's leadership abilities and hampering women in their bid for the governor's seat.

Overall, women in both senate and gubernatorial races campaign by illustrating their possession of "male" traits, since citizens value these traits in their leaders. However, in press coverage of both types of contests, reporters ignore the strategies of women candidates. In senate races, reporters actually allocate less attention to "male" traits than "female" traits, reversing the preferences of women senate candidates. Furthermore, female reporters are less likely than male reporters to use "male" traits to describe women running for U.S. senator. When covering women candidates for governor, reporters are less likely than women candidates to use "male" adjectives in their press reports. However, reporters do rely on "male" traits more than "female" traits, and men and women reporters are equally likely to use these terms when describing women gubernatorial candidates.

While male and female candidates for governor do not receive the same treatment by the press, the gender differences in news coverage in gubernatorial campaigns are neither as consistent nor as dramatic as the gender differences in news patterns found in senate campaigns. Unlike their counterparts in senate campaigns, for example, men and women receive approximately the same amount of press coverage in gubernatorial campaigns.

In addition, the discussion of the horse race is not consistently greater for women gubernatorial candidates than for their male colleagues. Furthermore, women candidates for governor are not always described by the press as less viable than male candidates. Finally, the discussion of campaign resources is not primarily negative, as it is for women senate candidates. In fact, more attention is given to the positive assets of women candidates than male candidates for governor.

While the gender differences in news coverage are less striking in gubernatorial races, men and women candidates do not receive identical coverage in local newspapers. First, as with their counterparts in senate races, the policy priorities of women candidates receive less attention in the news. Reporters in both senate and gubernatorial contests allocate significantly less space to the coverage of issues for women candidates. Instead, reporters concentrate on the horse race for women senate candidates and on personality characteristics for women gubernatorial candidates.

Second, the campaign agendas of women gubernatorial candidates and women senate candidates are reproduced less faithfully than the agendas of their male counterparts. For example, women candidates for governor demonstrate their competence for dealing with "male" issues such as the economy in their political advertisements. However, reporters—and especially women reporters—focus more heavily on "female" issues such as education and health care when covering these candidates. Similarly, reporters are less likely than women candidates to use "male" adjectives to describe women running for governor and senator. In contrast, reporters use the same types of traits as male candidates do when following their campaigns for statewide office.

In the next chapter I examine how differences in the press coverage of male and female gubernatorial candidates influence the candidates' chances of election. I use the experimental design introduced in chapter 5 to examine the impact of press patterns in gubernatorial campaigns. I simulate the coverage patterns found in the content analysis of gubernatorial campaigns to test whether these differences influence people's views of male and female candidates for governor.

8

News Coverage and Gender in Gubernatorial Campaigns: An Experimental Study of the Female Candidate's "Potential" Advantage

✵

Women candidates are much more likely to run successful gubernatorial campaigns than senate campaigns. The quality of the media attention accorded to women could be partially responsible for these differences in success rates. While women senate candidates receive less coverage and the coverage that they do receive is less favorable than that of their male counterparts, gender differences in news attention are less impressive in gubernatorial races. The news media, a significant obstacle for women senate candidates, could be less of a hindrance for women running for governor.

While gender differences in news coverage are likely to be less powerful in gubernatorial races than senate races, the impact of sex stereotypes may be more important in gubernatorial campaigns. Since men and women candidates for governor are treated similarly by the press, voters cannot rely as heavily on the news media to draw distinctions between the candidates. Instead, voters are likely to turn to sex stereotypes to help differentiate between the candidates.

In addition to playing a powerful role in gubernatorial races, sex stereotypes could also produce more favorable impressions of female candidates. Since people's reliance on stereotypes leads them to view women as more competent at handling "female" issues, and because these issues are more prominent in gubernatorial contests, women gubernatorial candidates are likely to be advantaged by voters' stereotypes. In contrast, the salient issues in senate races rarely correspond with women's perceived strengths, thereby limiting the benefits women receive from people's stereotypical images of their candidacies.

The Experiment

I again use the experimental design introduced in chapter 5 to examine the impact of gender differences in news coverage on people's evaluations of male and female candidates for governor. In this experiment I recreate the patterns of press coverage found in the content analysis of gubernatorial campaigns and examine whether these patterns of coverage influence people's perceptions of the candidates. With this experimental design we can also examine the impact of sex stereotypes. By holding news coverage constant and giving people identical information about male and female candidates, we can see whether people rely on sex stereotypes to draw distinctions between identical candidates for governor. Finally, we can examine the cumulative impact of gender differences in coverage and of sex stereotypes on people's impressions of male and female gubernatorial candidates.

Development of Prototype Articles

To develop the prototype articles for the experiment, I used the findings from the content analysis of gubernatorial coverage. I created six newspaper articles that represented six distinct coverage patterns: male incumbent coverage, female incumbent coverage, male challenger coverage, female challenger coverage, male coverage in an open race, female coverage in an open race.[1] As in the senate experiment, a total of fourteen characteristics of coverage were varied to create the six gubernatorial articles: four characteristics relate to the amount and prominence of coverage (e.g., length of article), six relate to general elements of campaign coverage (e.g., amount of horse race coverage), three relate to candidate characteristics and candidate resources (e.g., mention of candidate qualifications), and one indicates the author's gender. Table 8.1 shows the coverage characteristics represented in the six gubernatorial articles.

The following examples will illustrate how gender differences in gubernatorial press coverage are represented in the six prototype articles. First, the content analysis of news coverage shows that male incumbents and challengers receive more issue coverage than their female counterparts. These differences, based on the average number of issue paragraphs per article, are represented in the prototype articles. For example, the content analysis revealed that an average of two and a half paragraphs about issues are contained in articles about male gubernatorial incumbents, while on average only two "issue" paragraphs are published in articles about female gubernatorial incumbents. For

TABLE 8.1
Summary of Differences in the Six Gubernatorial Articles

Coverage Characteristic	Male Incumbent Prototype Article	Female Incumbent Prototype Article
Length of Article	17 paragraphs	14 paragraphs
Paragraphs about Candidate	7 paragraphs	5 paragraphs
Prominence	Headline and Lead Mention	No Headline or Lead Mention
Location	Page 10	Page 5
Issues	2.5 Paragraphs	2 Paragraphs
Content of Issues	1 "Male" /1.5 "Female" (Taxes, Education)	1 "Male"/ 1 "Female" (Taxes, Education)
Horse Race Coverage	1 Paragraph	1/2 Paragraph
Horse Race Assessment	"Likely Winner"	"Likely Winner"
Criticism	2 Criticisms	2 Criticisms
Positive and Negative Resources	1 Positive Resource	1 Positive Resource
Traits Mentioned in Article	None	"Untrustworthy"
Headline Tone	Neutral	Mixture (Positive and Negative Tone)
Article Tone	Neutral	Mixture (Positive and Negative Tone)
Sex of Author	Male	Male

Coverage Characteristic	Male Challenger Prototype Article	Female Challenger Prototype Article
Length of Article	17 paragraphs	14 paragraphs
Paragraphs about Candidate	5 paragraphs	5 paragraphs
Prominence	No Headline or Lead Mention	No Headline or Lead Mention
Location	Page 10	Page 5
Issues	2 Paragraphs	1 Paragraph
Content of Issues	1 "Male" /1 "Female" (Taxes, Education)	.5 "Male"/.5 "Female" (Taxes, Education)
Horse Race Coverage	1/2 Paragraph	1 Paragraph
Horse Race Assessment	"Not Very Competitive"	"Somewhat Competitive"
Criticism	1 Criticism	1 Criticism
Positive and Negative Resources	1 Mixture of Resources	2 Mixture of Resource
Traits Mentioned in Article	None	"Strong"
Headline Tone	Not Mentioned in Headline	Not Mentioned in Headline
Article Tone	Negative/Mixed	Neutral
Sex of Author	Male	Male

Coverage Characteristic	Male Open Prototype Article	Female Open Prototype Article
Length of Article	16 paragraphs	15 paragraphs
Paragraphs about Candidate	6 paragraphs	6 paragraphs
Prominence	Headline and Lead Mention	Headline and Lead Mention
Location	Page 8	Page 10
Issues	2 Paragraphs	2 Paragraphs
Content of Issues (Taxes, Education)	1 "Male" /1 "Female"	2 "Male (Taxes)
Horse Race Coverage	1/2 Paragraph	1 Paragraph
Horse Race Assessment	"Competitive"	"Somewhat Competitive"
Criticism	2 Criticisms	1.5 Criticisms
Positive and Negative Resources	1 Positive Resource	2 Positive Resource
Traits Mentioned in Article	"Strong Leader"	"Strong Leader"
Headline Tone	Neutral	Neutral
Article Tone	Neutral	Neutral
Sex of Author	Male	Male

challengers, two paragraphs per article, on average, discuss male candidates' issue priorities, while only one paragraph, on average, details the policy concerns of female challengers. These differences are represented in the incumbent and challenger prototype articles.

The content analysis also suggested that the substance of the issue discussion varies with the candidates' gender, with reporters discussing "female" issues more when covering male candidates and "male" issues more when following the campaigns of women candidates. These gender differences in news coverage are most impressive for candidates competing in open races. In open races coverage of women candidates focus on "male" issues almost two-thirds of the time (63% of the time), while "male" issues are discussed significantly less often for their male colleagues (43% of the time). I represent these differences in the prototype articles for candidates in open races. In the prototype article representing coverage of male candidates in open races, the discussion of issues includes both "male" and "female" issues. In selecting the specific issues, I chose those that received the most press attention: taxes and education. In the prototype article representing coverage of female candidates in open races, the discussion of issues focuses exclusively on "male" issues and specifically on the issue of taxes, since this issue was mentioned more frequently than any other.

Design of Experiment

Using a 2 x 6 factorial design, I conducted an experiment to examine whether gender differences in news coverage and the candidates' sex influence people's

TABLE 8.2
Description of Experimental Conditions

Gubernatorial Experiment			
1	Male Incumbent Coverage	+	Male Candidate
2	Male Incumbent Coverage	+	Female Candidate
3	Female Incumbent Coverage	+	Male Candidate
4	Female Incumbent Coverage	+	Female Candidate
5	Male Challenger Coverage	+	Male Candidate
6	Male Challenger Coverage	+	Female Candidate
7	Female Challenger Coverage	+	Male Candidate
8	Female Challenger Coverage	+	Female Candidate
9	Male Candidate Coverage in Open Race	+	Male Candidate
10	Male Candidate Coverage in Open Race	+	Female Candidate
11	Female Candidate Coverage in Open Race	+	Male Candidate
12	Female Candidate Coverage in Open Race	+	Female Candidate

perceptions of male and female candidates for governor. As in the senate experiment, two factors were manipulated in the experiment: the candidate's sex (male or female) and the type of news coverage (male incumbent coverage, female incumbent coverage, male challenger coverage, female challenger coverage, male open coverage, female open coverage) represented by the six prototype articles.[2] A description of the resulting twelve experimental conditions is presented in table 8.2.

Experimental Procedure

As discussed in chapter 2, selected residents of Tempe, Arizona, volunteered for this study, which lasted approximately one hour. Participants came to a research setting on the Arizona State University campus, and they were randomly assigned to one of the twelve experimental conditions.[3] In each condition participants read a newspaper page that included one of the twelve prototype articles as well as two other political articles. After participants finished reading the entire newspaper page, they completed a questionnaire.[4]

Results

The Influence of News Coverage on Evaluations of Gubernatorial Candidates

While the news media clearly differentiate between male and female candidates in their coverage of U.S. Senate campaigns, gender differences in media treatment are less dramatic and less consistent in gubernatorial campaigns. Since the media's treatment of men and women candidates for governor is more equitable, coverage patterns are less likely to produce striking differences in perceptions of male and female gubernatorial candidates. The results of the two-way (coverage X gender) analyses of variance confirm this expectation; the gubernatorial articles produce differences in evaluations for only five of the eleven dimensions examined. Differences in coverage patterns, as represented by the prototype articles, influence assessments of the candidate's viability, compassion, and leadership ability. Variations in coverage are also related to assessments of the candidate's ability to deal with defense issues and education issues.[5]

To investigate the impact of news coverage more thoroughly, we can examine whether impressions of candidates of the same status diverge when these candidates are treated differently by the press. First, the data in table 8.3 indi-

TABLE 8.3
The Impact of Coverage on Evaluations of the Gubernatorial Candidates

Question[1]	Male Incumbent Coverage[2] (Mean)	Female Incumbent Coverage (Mean)	T Value[3]	D.F.[4]
Viability[**]	1.54	2.10	−3.72	98

Question	Male Challenger Coverage (Mean)	Female Challenger Coverage (Mean)	T Value	DF
Honesty[*]	2.02	2.34	−2.25	90
Military[*]	3.89	3.48	2.05	92

Question	Male Coverage in Open Races (Mean)	Female Coverage in Open Races (Mean)	T Value	DF
Compassion[*]	2.06	2.60	−2.63	87
Education[**]	2.40	3.21	−3.75	90

[1] See appendix 6 for exact question wordings.
[2] The smaller the number, the more positive the evaluation.
[3] One-tailed p values are presented for the issues explicitly mentioned in the coverage since coverage differences lead us to expect a directional difference in evaluations. Issues explicitly mentioned in the articles are viability assessments for all conditions and education assessments in the open race conditions. Two-tailed p values are presented for all other traits and issues.
[4] D.F. stands for degrees of freedom.
[*] p<.05
[**] p<.01

cate that gender differences in news coverage are largely inconsequential for male and female governors. Unlike senate campaigns, where gender differences in incumbent coverage influence evaluations along a wide range of dimensions, gender differences in coverage of gubernatorial incumbents affect only one dimension: viability assessments. Candidates who are covered in the news as female incumbents are considered less electable than candidates receiving male incumbent coverage.[6]

While gender differences in viability coverage hurt female governors, female challengers do not face this same obstacle. In fact, according to the content analysis findings, women challengers are often described as somewhat more competitive than male challengers. However, this potential advantage in coverage patterns fails to influence evaluations, perhaps because the horse race receives little press attention in races with gubernatorial challengers. As the data in table 8.3 indicate, gender differences in coverage patterns fail to influence people's judgments about the electability of men and women challengers.

Although press patterns do not influence viability assessments of challengers, other gender differences in news treatment do produce some important differences in evaluations. In particular, candidates who receive male challenger coverage are viewed as more honest, while candidates covered as female challengers are considered better able to deal with defense issues. These differences in evaluations are not tied to explicit differences in the content of the prototype articles. Instead, the two articles produce distinct images of the candidates which influence people's views of the candidates.[7]

Candidates covered as female challengers are viewed as better able to deal with defense issues. However, this evaluation advantage is likely to be unimportant since foreign policy is rarely mentioned during gubernatorial campaigns (only 1 percent of all gubernatorial articles mention these issues). In contrast, the coverage advantage that male challengers enjoy is potentially important. Candidates receiving male challenger coverage are viewed as more honest; since voters often consider a candidate's integrity when developing overall impressions of candidates, this characteristic of press coverage is likely to benefit male challengers.

Finally, in open races male and female candidates are treated differently by the news media and these differences influence impressions of the candidates. In particular, candidates receiving male coverage are seen as more compassionate and better able to deal with education issues (see table 8.3). While the advantage in education assessments is directly tied to differences in the male and female prototype articles, differences in perceptions of the candidate's compassion cannot be explained by specific differences in the prototype articles. Instead, candidates covered as male candidates may be viewed as more compassionate precisely because they are more interested in education rather than economic issues.

Overall, differences in the way journalists cover men and women candidates are less dramatic in gubernatorial races than in senate races. However, distinctions in coverage do exist and these differences consistently lead people to develop more positive impressions of candidates receiving male candidate coverage. Regardless of their status, candidates in gubernatorial races who are covered as male candidates are viewed more favorably along a series of dimensions.

The Influence of Candidate Gender: Sex Stereotyping

In developing impressions of candidates, people rely on the media to draw distinctions between competing candidates. Because the press provide information about each candidate's personal characteristics, viability, and issue concerns, the news media influence how people view candidates. In addition to evaluating the media's presentation, people could consider the candidates' gender when developing impressions of competing candidates. Sex stereotypes are likely to benefit female gubernatorial candidates, just as they advantage women in senate contests. However, the significance of sex stereotypes is likely to be greater in races for governor. While women in senate races are seen as better able to deal with education and health issues, these advantages are not significant, since these issues rarely topped the agenda in U.S. Senate campaigns in the 1980s. In gubernatorial races, on the other hand, education and health issues are often important, and people's reliance on sex stereotypes will produce important advantages for women gubernatorial candidates.

As the data in table 8.4 indicate, sex stereotypes are pervasive in gubernatorial races. People rely on the candidates' gender to differentiate between equivalent candidates, and these distinctions always produce more positive impressions of women candidates. With regard to issues, women are considered better able to handle education, health, and women's issues. Female candidates, for instance, are viewed as competent (2.36) at dealing with education issues, while men are considered only somewhat competent (2.98)

In addition, and unexpectedly, women are seen as better able to deal with farm issues. People's reliance on stereotypes also leads them to view women as

TABLE 8.4
The Impact of Sex Stereotypes on Evaluations of the Gubernatorial Candidates

Question[1]	Male Candidate[2] (Mean)	Female Candidate (Mean)	T Value[3]	D.F.[4]
Compassion**	2.64	1.91	7.24	270
Education**	2.98	2.36	5.07	279
Health**	3.42	2.86	4.55	247
Honesty**	2.56	2.00	6.36	271
Honesty and Integrity**	3.32	2.56	6.40	264
Women**	3.73	2.45	10.89	249
Economy	3.41	3.18	1.87	265
Farm**	3.48	3.14	2.87	246
Knowledge**	2.53	2.20	3.90	281
Leadership**	2.59	2.37	2.04	265
Military	3.68	3.52	1.38	257

[1] See appendix 6 for exact question wordings.
[2] The smaller the number, the more positive the evaluation.
[3] Two-tailed p values are presented for all traits and issues.
[4] D.F. stands for degrees of freedom.
* p<.05
** p<.01

more compassionate, more honest, and better able to maintain honesty and integrity in government. Finally, women have an advantage along two traditionally male dimensions. Counter to previous findings on stereotypes (e.g., Ashmore and Del Boca 1979; Broverman, Vogel, Broverman, Clarkson, and Rosenkrantz 1974), female gubernatorial candidates are considered more knowledgeable and stronger leaders than their male counterparts.

These stereotypical advantages are pervasive, impressive, and likely to be influential. Besides the substantial benefits that women enjoy in salient issue domains such as education and health policy, women candidates for governor are also aided along important trait dimensions. People consider the candidate's competence and integrity when choosing between potential candidates, and these experimental results show that women hold important advantages along each of these dimensions.

Since people rely on gender schemas to process deficient or ambiguous information (e.g., Bem 1981; Markus, Crane, Bernstein, and Saldi 1982; Martin 1987), the frequency of stereotyping is likely to be affected by the qual-

TABLE 8.5A
The Pattern of Sex Stereotypes by Coverage Condition: Senate Candidates

Question[1]	Male Incumbent[2] (Condition 1 + Condition 3)	Female Incumbent (Condition 2 + Condition 4)	T Value[3]	D.F.
Not Mentioned in Articles	(Mean)	(Mean)		
Education**	3.43	2.92	2.02	43
Honesty**	2.82	2.17	3.23	44
Women**	3.70	2.20	5.42	43
Question[1]	Male Challenger (Condition 5 + Condition 7)	Female Challenger (Condition 6 + Condition 8)	T Value[3]	D.F.[4]
Not Mentioned in Articles	(Mean)	(Mean)		
Education**	3.43	2.92	2.02	43
Honesty**	2.82	2.17	3.23	44
Women**	3.70	2.20	5.42	43
Mentioned in Article(s)	(Mean)	(Mean)		
Honesty**	3.36	2.39	3.58	30

[1] See appendix 6 for exact question wordings.
[2] The smaller the number, the more positive the evaluation.
[3] Two-tailed p values are presented for all traits and issues.
[4] D.F. stands for degrees of freedom.
* p<.05
** p<.01

TABLE 8.5B
The Pattern of Sex Stereotypes by Coverage Condition: Gubernatorial Candidates

Question[1]	Male Incumbent[2] (Condition 1 + Condition 3)	Female Incumbent (Condition 2 + Condition 4)	T Value[3]	D.F.[4]
Not Mentioned				
in Articles	(Mean)	(Mean)		
Compassion[**]	2.48	1.89	3.23	86
Health[**]	3.51	2.77	3.27	76
Knowledgeable[**]	2.51	2.06	3.13	94
Women[**]	3.70	2.20	5.42	43
Mentioned				
in Article(s)	(Mean)	(Mean)		
Education[**]	2.69	2.15	2.32	90
Honesty[**]	2.58	1.98	3.85	89

Question	Male Challenger (Condition 5 + Condition 7)	Female Challenger (Condition 6 + Condition 8)	T Value	DF
Not Mentioned				
in Articles	(Mean)	(Mean)		
Compassion[**]	2.57	2.02	3.38	93
Honesty and Integrity[*]	3.16	2.78	3.67	88
Women[**]	3.62	2.50	6.42	86

Question	Male in Open Races (Condition 9 + Condition 11)	Female in Open Races (Condition 10 + Condition 12)	T Value	DF
Not Mentioned				
in Articles	(Mean)	(Mean)		
Compassion[**]	2.88	1.80	6.04	87
Health[**]	3.57	2.78	3.67	79
Honest[**]	2.81	1.94	5.80	88
Honesty and Integrity[**]	3.63	2.36	6.50	88
Knowledge[**]	2.56	2.26	2.00	89
Women[**]	3.95	2.40	7.84	79
Mentioned				
in Article(s)	(Mean)	(Mean)		
Education[**]	3.34	2.25	5.38	90
Leadership[**]	2.93	2.34	3.20	86

[1] See appendix 6 for exact question wordings.
[2] The smaller the number, the more positive the evaluation.
[3] Two-tailed p values are presented for all traits and issues.
[4] D.F. stands for degrees of freedom.
[*] p<.05
[**] p<.01

ity of information available to voters. In particular, in the experimental setting stereotyping is more likely to occur for issues and traits not discussed in the news articles. By looking at specific coverage comparisons in both senate and gubernatorial contests, we can see whether people rely on sex stereotypes to fill in information gaps.

As the data in table 8.5 demonstrate, respondents are much more likely to stereotype when they are given no information on a particular topic. Thirteen of the seventeen instances of stereotyping occur for topics not mentioned in the newspaper articles. For instance, people reading about gubernatorial incumbents are provided with no details about either candidate's concern for health issues. Therefore, when asked to evaluate the candidates' ability to deal with health policy, respondents rely on their stereotypical images of men and women, which leads them to develop more favorable views of female incumbents. Among senatorial incumbents, in contrast, the prototype article representing female incumbent coverage does mention the candidate's concern for health-related issues. Since they are given this information, respondents have no need to rely on sex stereotypes when evaluating the candidates receiving incumbent coverage; consistent with this expectation, there is no evidence of stereotyping to be found here.

Finally, certain types of respondents may be more likely to use stereotypes. As in the senate case, the gender schema of women respondents could be more accessible, encouraging women to use stereotypes more frequently to distinguish between equivalent male and female candidates. Or, women may be more likely than men to adopt certain feminist beliefs regarding the unique qualities that women bring to politics. If this is the case, women will be more willing than men to use gender as a way of drawing distinctions between similar men and women candidates.

Although gender differences in the application of stereotypes are less dramatic in the case of a gubernatorial race, women continue to use sex stereotypes more frequently than male respondents. While men distinguish between equivalent male and female candidates along seven of the eleven dimensions examined, women use stereotypes to differentiate between the candidates along nine dimensions. Women respondents, unlike their male counterparts, consider female candidates more competent at dealing with farm issues, and they also consider female candidates stronger leaders.

The results of these experiments demonstrate that people frequently rely on sex stereotypes, and these stereotypes always produce more positive impressions of women candidates. In gubernatorial races, unlike senate contests, the substance of these stereotypes is likely to be influential. In races for governor, issues related to health care and education are prominent, and, therefore, people's reliance on stereotypes will produce important electoral advantages for women candidates. In addition, stereotypes influence people's evaluations of the personal characteristics of gubernatorial candidates, with women gubernatorial candidates being viewed as stronger leaders, more knowledgeable, and more honest than equivalent male candidates. Because they are often linked to overall evaluations of candidates, these traits are likely to help women in their gubernatorial bids.

The Influence of Candidate Gender and Coverage

Stereotypical images of men and women lead people to develop more positive images of women gubernatorial candidates. In contrast, the impact of coverage differences, although less pervasive, tends to provide male candidates with an advantage. Since gender differences in press treatment as well as people's reliance on sex stereotypes independently influence people's views of gubernatorial candidates, we need to assess the cumulative impact of these two factors. By examining the joint impact of stereotypes and press patterns, we can simulate a campaign where the candidate's gender and press coverage are naturally tied.

In gubernatorial races gender differences in news coverage often conflict with people's stereotypes. For example, candidates covered as male challengers are viewed as more honest than candidates who receive female challenger coverage, yet people's stereotypes lead them to view female candidates as more honest. Similarly, while stereotypes encourage people to view women as better equipped to deal with education issues, candidates covered as male candidates in open races are seen as more competent at dealing with educational issues. This conflict between press patterns and stereotypes could diminish the impact of stereotypes, thereby depriving women gubernatorial candidates of an important electoral resource.

The data in table 8.6 display the cumulative impact of coverage differences and sex stereotypes on people's views of male and female gubernatorial candidates. Women gubernatorial candidates, unlike their counterparts in senate races, are not at a disadvantage as the result of coverage patterns. Some of the coverage differences found earlier are less influential here because they contradict people's stereotypical images. For instance, while candidates covered as male candidates in open races are viewed as more compassionate (see table

TABLE 8.6
The Cumulative Impact of Candidate Gender and Candidate Coverage on Evaluations of the Gubernatorial Candidates

Question[1]	Male Incumbent Coverage with Male Candidate[2] (Mean)	Female Incumbent Coverage with Female Candidate (Mean)	T Value[3]	D.F.
Coverage Effects				
Viability	1.65	1.92	−1.13	47
Gender Effects				
Compassion**	2.54	1.96	2.25	44
Education*	2.73	2.20	1.78	45
Health*	3.47	2.80	1.93	37
Honesty**	2.65	1.96	3.19	42
Honesty and Integrity**	3.30	2.56	2.18	41
Knowledge**	2.52	1.96	2.61	41
Women**	3.74	2.43	4.04	40

Question	Male Challenger Coverage with Male Candidate (Mean)	Female Challenger Coverage with Female Candidate (Mean)	T Value	D.F[4]
Coverage Effects				
Military	3.95	3.54	1.53	44
Honesty	2.14	2.25	−0.57	43
Gender Effects				
Compassion	2.52	2.19	1.40	45
Honesty and Integrity	3.04	2.87	0.80	43
Women***	3.45	2.56	3.90	41

Question	Male Coverage in Open Race with Male Candidate (Mean)	Female Coverage in Open Race with Female Candidate (Mean)	T Value	D.F.
Coverage Effects				
Education	2.87	2.57	1.07	42
Gender Effects				
Compassion**	2.67	2.09	2.19	40
Health*	3.37	2.81	1.73	38
Honesty***	2.71	2.00	3.25	42
Honesty and Integrity***	3.59	2.50	3.67	42
Knowledge	2.54	2.24	1.40	41
Leadership**	2.90	2.31	2.23	40
Women***	3.68	2.52	3.91	38

[1] See appendix 6 for exact question wordings.
[2] The smaller the number, the more positive the evaluation.
[3] One-tailed p values are presented for the issues explicitly mentioned in the coverage since coverage differences lead us to expect a directional difference in evaluations. Issues explicitly mentioned in the articles are viability assessments for all conditions and education assessments in the open race conditions. Two-tailed p values are presented for all other traits and issues.
[4] D.F. stands for degrees of freedom.
* p<.10
** p<.05
*** p<.01

8.4), this advantage in evaluations disappears when it clashes with people's stereotypical views of men and women.

People's reliance on sex stereotypes, on the other hand, leads respondents to develop more favorable images of women candidates. Women governors, for instance, when compared to their male counterparts, are viewed as more compassionate, more honest, and better able to deal with education, health, and women's issues.

While continuing to be an important resource for women candidates, stereotypes are less powerful when they compete with coverage patterns. Female incumbents and female candidates in open races, for example, are viewed as more honest and better able to maintain honesty and integrity in government, but women challengers do not enjoy this advantage. Women challengers are not viewed as favorably along these dimensions because coverage patterns present conflicting information. In particular, male challengers are described in the news as honest, while their female counterparts are not portrayed in this fashion.

Overall, female candidates for governor are in an enviable position when compared with their counterparts in senate races. Gender differences in news coverage are less impressive and do not encourage people to develop more negative impressions of women candidates. In addition, the impact of stereotypes, which consistently advantage women, are more powerful in gubernatorial races.

The Influence of Candidate Status

In developing images of gubernatorial candidates, voters consider the sex of the candidates and the way that the candidates are covered by the press. In addition, the candidates' status is likely to influence voters' views of competing candidates for governor. While the role of incumbency has received more attention in congressional elections than in gubernatorial elections, several studies have examined the importance of status in races for governor. These survey studies suggest that while incumbency plays a less powerful role in gubernatorial races than in senate races, the impact of incumbency remains important (Chubb 1980; Piereson 1977; Seroka 1980; Wright 1974).

As I discussed in chapter 5, congressional scholars have suggested that incumbency per se does not matter; rather, incumbents are more successful than challengers because they are better known and better liked than their opponents (Jacobson 1987). I test this contention experimentally, as in the senate case, by comparing evaluations of incumbents (male and female) with nonincumbents (male and female). If differences in evaluations emerge, these differences either reflect variations in news patterns for incumbents and non-incumbents or they reflect the impact of status (i.e., incumbency per se).

In senate races people appear to rely on prototypes to distinguish between incumbents and challengers. For instance, respondents considered incum-bents to be stronger leaders, and they expressed a greater willingness to vote for incumbent candidates (see chapter 5). In gubernatorial races incumbents enjoy similar advantages. As the data in table 8.7 indicate, participants consis-tently evaluate incumbents more positively than nonincumbents (challengers and candidates in open races).

While incumbent governors have an advantage along a number of dimen-sions, some of the advantages are due to differences in news coverage, while others illustrate pure status effects. The difference in viability assessments, for example, is likely to be driven by differences in press treatment. Governors running for reelection are consistently viewed by the press as more electable than nonincumbents, and this difference in news coverage encourages people to consider sitting governors more electable.

TABLE 8.7
The Impact of Candidate Status on Evaluations of the Gubernatorial Candidates

Question[1]	Incumbent[2] (Mean)	Challenger (Mean)	T Value[3]	D.F.[4]
Education[*]	2.41	2.79	-2.49	187
Leadership[**]	2.18	2.63	-3.55	177
Viability[**]	1.83	2.61	-7.71	202
Vote[*]	2.67	2.58	-2.50	176

Question[1]	Incumbent[2] (Mean)	Candidate in Open Race (Mean)	T Value[3]	D.F.
Defense[*]	3.40	3.72	-2.24	164
Education[*]	1.83	2.16	-3.27	192
Leadership[**]	2.41	2.63	-3.55	177
Viability[**]	1.83	2.77	-2.16	182
Vote[*]	2.27	2.52	-2.05	164

[1] See appendix 6 for exact question wordings.
[2] The smaller the number, the more positive the evaluation.
[3] Two-tailed p values are presented for all traits and issues.
[4] D.F. stands for degrees of freedom.
[*] $p < .05$
[**] $p < .01$

Other advantages in evaluations are not driven exclusively by news patterns. For example, governors are seen as better able to deal with education issues than challengers, yet this difference cannot be explained by variations in press coverage. In the articles describing incumbents and challengers, for example, education issues are always mentioned. Nevertheless, when we compare evaluations of incumbents and challengers, we find that incumbents are considered more competent than challengers at dealing with educational issues.

In addition, and more persuasively, incumbents are consistently viewed as stronger leaders than nonincumbents. In comparing incumbents and challengers, incumbents are viewed as stronger leaders than challengers, even though the leadership qualities of the candidates are never mentioned in these news articles. Similarly, incumbents are at an advantage when compared with candidates in open races, and this advantage is particularly striking since each article about open race candidates—and neither incumbent article—stresses the candidate's leadership qualities. These results suggest that incumbents are regarded as stronger leaders simply because they are sitting governors.

Finally, participants express a greater willingness to vote for incumbent candidates. This difference in vote intention is probably influenced both by content differences and by the candidates' status. Overall, these results show both that incumbents have a clear advantage over nonincumbents in terms of people's evaluations and that this advantage is driven by differences in press patterns *and* by the candidates' status. As in the senate case, these results suggest that incumbency acts as a cue for voters, supplying them with additional information about the candidates. This added information favors the incumbent, serving as an additional resource for governors. The incumbency advantage found here—both in terms of status and coverage—will hurt female gubernatorial candidates, who almost always run as nonincumbents. Between 1970 and 1992, 87 percent of the women gubernatorial candidates ran as nonincumbents.

The findings of this study suggest that people's perceptions of male and female candidates are influenced by both gender differences in media patterns and people's sex stereotypes. Yet the impact of press patterns and stereotypes differs for gubernatorial and senatorial candidates. Gender differences in press treatment are more dramatic in senate races and produce more negative impressions of female candidates. In gubernatorial races, by contrast, campaign coverage is more equitable and does not lead to impressive differences in evaluations of male and female candidates.

People's reliance on sex stereotypes to distinguish between equivalent men and women candidates consistently produces more positive evaluations of women candidates, with respondents using "female" stereotypes to draw distinctions between equivalent candidates. In addition, the pattern of stereotyping varies with the sex of the respondent and the content of the information available. Overall, the reliance on sex stereotypes works to the advantage of women candidates, leading respondents to develop more favorable images of these candidates.

Although stereotypes produce more favorable views of women candidates in senate and gubernatorial elections, these stereotypes are likely to be more important for women in gubernatorial contests. First, female candidates in senate and gubernatorial races are seen as better able to deal with social issues, such as health and education issues. Yet these issues are more salient and more important in gubernatorial races. Second, sex stereotyping along personality dimensions is more pervasive in gubernatorial races. Female candidates for governor, for example, are viewed as stronger leaders and more knowledgeable than equivalent male candidates, and these stereotypical advantages are likely to produce important electoral benefits.

While sex stereotypes help women gubernatorial candidates, the impact of these stereotypes is muted when they conflict with gender differences in news patterns. For instance, female gubernatorial challengers do not enjoy the same stereotypical advantages as female incumbents and female candidates in open races, because gender differences in challenger coverage clash with stereotypical images of male and female candidates.

Finally, women candidates in both U.S. Senate and gubernatorial elections are at a disadvantage due to their status as nonincumbents. The experimental results suggest that differences in news coverage and the candidates' status lead people to develop more favorable views of incumbents. For example, senators and governors are viewed as stronger leaders and more electable than candidates running as nonincumbents.

Overall, the results of this study suggest that the context of the election matters and that it provides women with opportunities in certain settings and obstacles in other settings. For the electoral period studied here, women candidates for governor enjoy more advantages than their colleagues in senate races. First, because gender differences in coverage are less dramatic in gubernatorial races, press coverage produces less negative images of female gubernatorial candidates. Second, the correspondence between the issue domains for these two offices and people's sex stereotypes yields an advantage to women running for governor. Women candidates for the U.S. Senate, on the other hand, are in a less enviable position.

While the context of the campaign influences the electability of women candidates, particular offices may not invariably produce obstacles (or advantages) for women. Since the salient issues and traits in campaigns are not static, the benefits enjoyed by women gubernatorial candidates and the barriers faced by senate candidates are not unalterable. During the 1992 senate campaigns, for instance, the end of the cold war made foreign policy issues less central and the concurrent presidential campaign made issues such as health care reform more prominent. Similarly, congressional scandals—such as the House banking scandal—made such traits as integrity and trustworthiness especially relevant. The context of the 1992 campaign, then, placed a premium on women's stereotypical strengths ("female" issues and "female" traits), thereby creating a favorable electoral setting for women candidates for the U.S. Senate.

In the next chapter I rely on survey data to examine the generalizability of the experimental findings. I also look at how changes in the context of the campaign influenced the electability of women candidates running for the U.S. Senate between 1988 and 1992.

9

The Electoral Consequences of Stereotypes

✺

In this chapter I analyze survey data to examine how variations in the campaign context—which either highlights or deemphasizes women candidates' stereotypical strengths—influence the likelihood of voters supporting women candidates. The findings of earlier chapters indicate that the context of the campaign mediates the impact of stereotypes on the behavior of voters, the news media, and the candidates. In this chapter I explicitly test whether the content of the electoral climate affects the electability of women candidates.

According to findings discussed earlier, the stereotypical advantages of women candidates along certain trait and issue dimensions are consequential only when these dimensions are salient to voters. Therefore, women senate candidates were not helped by voters' stereotypes during the 1980s because "female" issues did not top the senate agenda. In contrast, gubernatorial campaigns during this same period focused on "female" issues such as health care and education, which led voters to consider these "female" issues when comparing male and female candidates for governor. The salience of "female" issues, coupled with voters' stereotypes, created more favorable impressions of women gubernatorial candidates.

The news media respond to the context of the campaign when covering male and female candidates for statewide office. When there is a favorable correspondence between the campaign climate and peoples' stereotypical images of women candidates (e.g., races for governor in the 1980s), the news media treat women candidates more equitably. On the other hand, when the electoral climate highlights women's perceived weaknesses (e.g., races for senator in the 1980s), the press treat women candidates less fairly. For instance, in covering campaigns for the U.S. Senate, reporters gave women candidates less coverage, and the coverage they did receive was primarily negative and emphasized their unlikely chances of victory.

Finally, the candidates themselves consider the electoral environment when campaigning for statewide office. In the last decade women candidates running for the U.S. Senate competed in a campaign arena that emphasized their perceived vulnerabilities. In responding to this hostile setting, women senate candidates engaged in negative campaigning more frequently than their male colleagues. In contrast, women candidates in gubernatorial races competed in a more favorable electoral climate. This setting fueled a positive campaign strategy where women gubernatorial candidates relied more heavily than their male counterparts on positive advertisements.

Since the actions of the press, the candidates, and the voters are influenced by the correspondence between people's stereotypical images and the prevailing campaign environment, the context of the campaign is likely to affect the political fortunes of women candidates. By investigating voters' reactions to women candidates in different types of campaign settings, I can assess how the electability of women candidates is conditioned by the electoral climate.

The Data

To examine the electoral consequences of the campaign climate, I use the 1988–1992 National Election Study (NES)/Senate Election Study (SES). For the first time in 1988 and continuing through 1992, the National Election Study collected data on senate campaigns by interviewing approximately equal numbers of respondents from each state. Relying on NES/SES data, I develop a model to assess how the context of the campaign influences voters' evaluations of the twenty-one women who ran for the U.S. Senate between 1988 and 1992.[1]

By coupling the survey data with information about the context of the campaign, we can see whether a favorable correspondence between the campaign's major themes and women's perceived strengths encourages voters to view women candidates more favorably. Conversely, this investigation will illustrate whether a campaign setting that stresses women's perceived weaknesses produces lower levels of support for women candidates.

The present examination nicely complements the analyses I presented in earlier chapters. First, while the experiments ascertained participants' reactions to fictional candidates in a somewhat artificial setting, this survey measures respondents' assessments of authentic senate candidates in a real-life setting. In addition, since probability sampling methods are used to obtain the interviews, the respondents included in the survey study are a representative sample of citizens in senate elections. In contrast, the participants in the experiments were a varied sample of two local communities. Finally, the survey study extends the range of inquiry by looking at the impact of sex stereotypes in three more recent election cycles.

Supplementing the earlier studies with the survey study increases our understanding of the role of stereotypes in campaigns. The survey's strengths (e.g., generalizability) and weaknesses (e.g., ability to isolate causal variables) correspond to the weaknesses (e.g., generalizability) and strengths (e.g., ability to isolate causal variables) of the experimental method; by embracing "methodological pluralism," we reduce our dependence on any specific design and increase our confidence in the experimental findings.

The Dependent Variables

To investigate how the campaign setting influences people's assessment of women candidates, I rely on two dependent variables. First, the feeling thermometer is used to assess how warm or cold respondents' feelings are toward the female candidate, on a scale ranging from 0 to 100.[2] In addition, I look at whether respondents say they voted for the female candidate.[3] These measures, although highly correlated, are not identical.[4] For example, respondents who give a woman candidate high ratings on the feeling thermometer may not vote for the candidate if they give the woman's opponent an even higher rating.

Independent Variables

The Electoral Context

To see whether the electoral climate influenced people's reactions to women candidates, I supplemented the NES/SES survey data with a contextual variable measuring the campaign environment. I content analyzed reports on each senate campaign published in the *Congressional Quarterly*'s (CQ) preelection issue. These reports characterize the ongoing campaign by describing the competing candidates' strategies, their political resources, and the likely outcome of each race. In the content analysis I listed the issues and traits mentioned by the reporter and calculated the proportion of "female" and "male" themes.[5] This measure of the campaign environment can take on any value between 0 (all "male" themes) and 1.0 (all "female" themes).[6]

Between 1988 and 1992, "male" themes were slightly more common than "female" themes (mean=.48 with a standard deviation of .21) in the campaigns of women candidates.[7] Jean Lloyd-Jones, in her uphill battle against incumbent Charles Grassley, participated in the most "male"-oriented campaign (.11), while Patty Murray, who described herself as a "mother, teacher, and day care worker" (CQ [1992]:3353), ran successfully in the most "female"-oriented campaign (.83).

Contrary to popular impressions, "female" themes were not significantly more widespread in 1992 as compared to 1988 and 1990. In fact, the campaign conducted in 1988 had slightly more "female" themes (mean=.60) than the campaigns contested in 1992 (mean=.52 with a standard deviation of .25) or 1990 (mean=.43 with a standard deviation of .17).

However, the races contested between 1988 and 1992 were significantly more "female"-oriented than the campaigns contested between 1982 and 1986 (mean=.32 with a standard deviation of .22).[8] Three races during the earlier time period included no reference to "female" themes and no campaign during this period mentioned more "female" than "male" themes. As an illustration, CQ offered the following description of the 1984 Minnesota race between the incumbent, Rudy Boschwitz, and Joan Growe:

> Growe has taken a page from Mondale in describing the Senate campaign as a battle between two visions of the future. And like the former vice president, she includes in her vision the prospect of increased taxes (particularly among the wealthy) and spending cuts to curtail the huge budget deficits. She has also sought to tap into the state's strong nuclear freeze movement.
>
> (CQ [1986]:2553).

"Male" themes in U.S. Senate races were less prevalent in the 1988–1992 period as compared to the 1984–1986 period. The elimination of the nuclear arms race and the breakdown of the Soviet Union freed candidates to talk about other pressing issues such as education and the environment. For example, in 1992 Barbara Boxer called for a "full agenda of environmental protections and social liberties from abortion rights to gay rights" in her successful campaign for California's U.S. Senate seat (CQ [1992]:3345). Similarly, Geri Rothman-Serot of Missouri talked "passionately about the need for universal health care" (CQ [1992]:3348) while campaigning for the U.S. Senate in 1992.

While dramatic changes in world politics influenced the agendas of campaigns for the U.S. Senate, recent campaigns continue to vary in their emphases on "male" and "female" themes. In the present analysis I examine how variations in the campaign climate influence women's election to the U.S. Senate by looking at whether a favorable correspondence between people's stereotypical views and the climate of the campaign produces more positive evaluations of women candidates.

Control Variables

Although my primary objective is to see whether the campaign setting affects people's reactions to women candidates, it is necessary to control for rival factors. By including these rival variables in a comprehensive model of vote choice, we can see whether the campaign context continues to have an independent effect on the electability of women candidates. For example, I expect to find that women will be more successful in campaigns that highlight "female" issues, since such settings emphasize women candidates' stereotypical strengths. However, the relationship between the campaign setting and women's success may be spurious. For instance, the quality of the candidate may affect both (1) the campaign agenda and (2) the candidate's success. A strong woman candidate who can manipulate the agenda and focus attention on "female" issues may also be more successful in securing votes. If this is the case, the quality of the candidate rather than the campaign climate may influence the success of a woman's candidacy.

In developing the model of vote choice, I include five additional variables to measure the attitudes of voters and the characteristics of the candidates. Recent studies of senate elections show that each of these five variables influences voting decisions in U.S. Senate contests.

Attitudes of Voters

First, given that numerous scholars have documented the importance of party identification in Senate elections (Abramowitz 1980; Abramowitz and Segal 1990; Jacobson and Wolfinger 1989; Smith and Squire 1991; Wright and Berkman 1986), I include a measure of party affiliation in the vote model. In this study I use the standard seven-point scale[9] and recode respondents so that people who strongly identify with the woman candidate's party are given the highest score (+3), while respondents who strongly identify with the opposing candidate's party are given the lowest score (-3).

In addition, I look at the role of ideology in senate contests, since prior research demonstrates that voters consider the ideological positions of candidates when casting their votes (Abramowitz 1981; Abramowitz 1988; Abramowitz and Segal 1992; Westlye 1991; Wright and Berkman 1986). To examine the impact of ideology, I use the respondent's self-placement on the seven-point ideological scale, as well as the respondent's ideological placement of the woman candidate.[10] With these two measures I develop a variable assessing the respondent's ideological distance from the candidate, ranging from 0 to 6.[11]

Finally, people often consider the personality characteristics of the candidates when developing overall impressions of senate candidates (Abramowitz 1988; Goldenberg, Traugott, and Kahn 1987). To measure the impact of personal traits in senate elections, I use the open-ended likes/dislikes questions to develop a directional trait measure.[12] I sum the number of positive and negative trait comments mentioned for each woman candidate; the measure ranges from -4 to +4 for the 1988–1992 sample.[13]

Characteristics of the Candidates

Prior research illustrates the importance of the quality of the challenger by demonstrating that quality candidates are evaluated more positively than inexperienced candidates (Abramowitz 1988; Jacobson 1987; Smith and Squire 1991; Squire 1989; Stewart 1989). Quality candidates are likely to have stronger organizations, greater levels of funding, and better campaign skills than other candidates. As previous researchers have done, I develop a measure of challenger quality based on the challenger's prior political position. The measure ranges from 0 to 3, with 3 indicating House member or mayor of a major city; 2 indicating state legislator or city council member; 1 indicating former elected official or appointed official; and 0 indicating no previous governmental experience.

Finally, I include a measure of incumbency, since senate incumbents are better known and better liked than their nonincumbent counterparts (e.g., Jacobson 1987). During the 1988–1992 period, two women were incumbents: Barbara Mikulski of Maryland and Nancy Kassebaum of Kansas. I include a dummy variable that codes Mikulski and Kassebaum as 1 and the remaining candidates as 0.

While the NES/SES data allows us to see whether the context of the campaign influences people's views of women candidates, the survey instrument has some limitations. In particular, close-ended trait and issues questions are not included in the survey. Given this omission it is difficult to see whether the context of the campaign influences the impact of *specific* issues and traits on people's overall evaluations of the candidates. For instance, I expect that evaluations of a candidate's ability to deal with education issues will be weighed more heavily when education is a salient issue in the campaign, and women will have an advantage in such a campaign setting. Unfortunately, without the appropriate survey measures, we cannot examine the direct effect of specific issues and trait assessments on overall evaluations of women candidates.

Similarly, the survey analysis examines the outcome of stereotypes, not the process. While earlier chapters demonstrate that stereotypes influence the behavior of three types of political actors (journalists, candidates, and citizens), we cannot examine this process with the NES/SES data. Instead, we examine how the context of the campaign—which affects the actions of candidates, journalists, and citizens—influences voters' views of women candidates.

Results

To examine the impact of the campaign setting on the electability of women candidates, I begin by looking at the simple bivariate relationship between the content of campaign themes in the 1988–1992 senate campaigns and respondents' evaluations of women candidates. The significant correlation between feeling thermometer scores and the campaign setting ($r=.20$, $p<.01$) shows that people have favorable (or warm) attitudes toward women who run in campaigns highlighting "female" issues while their attitudes toward women competing in "male"-oriented environments are significantly cooler.

In addition, the relationship between the campaign's context and voters' feelings toward the candidate is higher for nonincumbents ($.23$, $p<.01$) than for incumbents ($-.03$, n.s.), which suggests that the election of nonincumbents is more dependent on the campaign climate. In contrast, incumbents seem to be more effective at successfully isolating themselves from an unfavorable environment. The incumbent's greater resources, voting history, and casework may create a public image that is largely independent of the current campaign. For instance, in 1990 Senator Nancy Kassebaum competed in a "male"-oriented setting where "male" themes were twice as common as "female" themes. However, running for her third term in the U.S. Senate,

A. Feeling Thermometer Scores

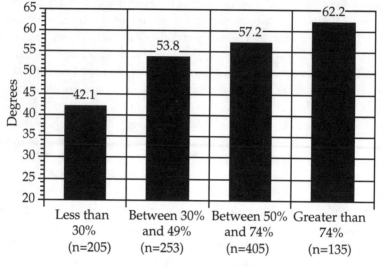

Percentage of "Female" Themes

B. Vote Preference

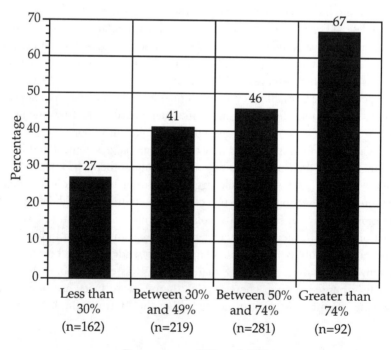

Percentage of "Female" Themes

Kassebaum received an average feeling thermometer score of 73 degrees, indicating the popularity of Kansas' junior senator.

A visual representation of the relationship between the campaign's context and people's attitudes toward women candidates is displayed in figure 9.1. The figure demonstrates that women have an advantage in races where their stereotypical strengths are emphasized. In campaigns where "female" themes accounted for about 75 percent of all themes, women received an average feeling thermometer score of 62 degrees. In contrast, when less than 30 percent of all the campaign themes were devoted to "female" issues and traits, women candidates were viewed much less warmly, receiving an average feeling thermometer score of 42 degrees.

An alternative way of assessing the impact of the campaign's context is to employ Ordinary Least Squares (OLS) regression analysis to look at the bivariate relationship between the climate of the campaign and citizens' feelings toward women candidates. This analysis, which produces an unstandardized coefficient of 23.77 with a standard error of 3.79, shows that the campaign's setting has a significant impact on people's views of women senate candidates. The coefficient indicates that women competing in campaigns dominated by all "female" themes are rated, on average, 24 degrees more warmly than women running in a climate featuring only "male" themes.

The context of the campaign also affects citizens' voting decisions. As illustrated in figure 9.1 (bottom panel), women receive much more support when their stereotypical strengths are highlighted by the campaign's climate. In campaigns where about three-quarters of the themes correspond to "female" themes, 67 percent of the respondents said that they intended to vote for the woman candidate. In contrast, in campaigns where "female" themes were less prominent, representing less than one-third of all themes, women received much lower levels of support. In these races only 27 percent of the respondents indicated support for the woman candidate.

The results of a bivariate logit regression also show that people express a greater willingness to vote for women running in campaigns stressing "female" themes. The logit coefficient (.97, with a standard error of .18) indicates that the campaign setting powerfully influences voters' choices for U.S. senator. In addition, the change in probability scores (Peterson 1985) shows that respondents are 23 percent more likely to vote for a woman candidate in a campaign dominated only by "female" themes, as compared with a campaign that contains only "male" themes.

While these results indicate a powerful bivariate relationship between the campaign's context and people's attitudes toward female candidates, it is important to determine whether the context remains influential when rival factors are examined. In table 9.1 I present a more fully specified model assessing people's views of women candidates. The results of this analysis show that the context of the campaign continues to affect people's evaluations of women candidates, even when standard determinants of the vote choice are included in the equation. The unstandardized regression coefficient (15.85) suggests that as one moves from a "male"-dominated campaign (context=0) to a campaign highlighting only "female" themes (context=1), people's positive feelings toward women candidates increase by more than 15 degrees. These results demonstrate that campaign settings that highlight women's stereotypical strengths act as an important resource for women candidates in U.S. Senate elections. In contrast, women are at a disadvantage when they compete in campaigns that highlight their stereotypical weaknesses.

TABLE 9.1

OLS Regression Equation Explaining Feeling Thermometer Scores for Women Senate Candidates

All Candidates		
Variable	Unstandardized Coefficient (SE)	Standardized Coefficient
Campaign Context[***]	15.85 (3.14)	.13
Party Identification[***]	2.38 (0.35)	.18
Ideology[***]	3.81 (0.49)	.21
Traits[***]	8.38 (0.69)	.32
Incumbency[***]	13.8 (2.00)	.18
Intercept[***]	46.74 (1.83)	
R^2	.35	
Number of Cases	998	

Nonincumbent Candidates		
Variable	Unstandardized Coefficient (SE)	Standardized Coefficient
Campaign Context[***]	17.30 (3.5)	.15
Party Identification[***]	2.34 (0.38)	.18
Ideology[***]	4.06 (0.52)	.24
Traits[***]	8.40 (0.79)	.31
Quality of Candidate[*]	1.15 (0.68)	.05
Intercept[***]	44.31 (2.11)	
R^2	.32	
Number of Cases	867	

[***] $p<.01$
[**] $p<.05$
[*] $p<.10$

In addition to considering the electoral climate, citizens' impressions of candidates are influenced by more traditional factors. For instance, people consider the candidate's party affiliation as well as ideological proximity when developing overall impressions of the candidates. Similarly, people's views of candidates are affected by their assessments of the candidates' personality characteristics. Finally, incumbents are evaluated significantly more favorably than nonincumbents; on average, citizens rate incumbents 14 points higher than nonincumbents.

Since the results of the bivariate analysis indicate that the campaign environment is more important for nonincumbents than incumbents, I examine the impact of campaign context—in the more fully specified model—focusing exclusively on challengers and candidates in open races. These results, also presented in table 9.1, show that the campaign setting is more important for women running as nonincumbents. For these candidates differences between an all "male" setting and an all "female" setting produce more than a 17-point change in feeling thermometer scores. The remaining attitudinal variables continue to be influential; party identification, ideology, and traits each affect citizens' overall evaluations of the candidates. In addition, the quality of the candidate, while less powerful, is positively related to people's assessments of women candidates.[14]

The context of the campaign clearly influences people's evaluations of women candidates. In addition, the data in table 9.2 demonstrate that the campaign setting affects people's voting decisions, with women receiving significantly more votes in races that spotlight their stereotypical strengths.[15] The change in probability score, listed in the second column, illustrates the importance of the context of the campaign. Controlling for all other factors, people are 18 percent more likely to vote for a woman running in a "female"-dominated campaign than for a woman running in a campaign featuring only "male" themes.

In addition, each of the traditional determinants of vote choice is also influential, with party having the most powerful effect on people's choices. Incumbency, as expected, is an important resource for sitting senators. Citizens are 27 percent more likely to vote for an incumbent than for a challenger or open race candidate. Overall, this vote model performs well—each of the logit coefficients is statistically significant, and the five variables predict 76 percent of the cases correctly.

The comparison of the two equations in table 9.2 demonstrates again that the context of the campaign is more important for challengers and candidates

TABLE 9.2
Logit Model Predicting the Vote for Women Senate Candidates

All Candidates Variable	Logit Coefficient (S.E.)	Change in Probability	Standardized Coefficient
Campaign Context***	.73 (.22)	.18	.32
Party Identification***	.27 (.03)	.06	1.09
Ideology***	.14 (.04)	.03	.40
Traits***	.29 (.05)	.07	.55
Incumbency***	1.15 (.18)	.27	.74
Intercept***	4.44 (1.13)		
Percent of Cases			
Correctly Predicted	76%		
Number of Cases	754		

Nonincumbent Candidates Variable	Logit Coefficient (S.E.)	Change in Probability	Standardized Coefficient
Campaign Context***	.92 (.24)	.23	.39
Party Identification***	.27 (.03)	.09	1.06
Ideology***	.15 (.04)	.01	.42
Traits***	.26 (.06)	.10	.45
Quality of Candidate	.05 (.05)	.01	.11
Intercept***	4.28 (1.5)		
Percent of Cases			
Correctly Predicted	74%		
Number of Cases	673		

*** $p < .01$

in open races. The logit coefficient and standardized coefficient in the nonincumbent model are larger, demonstrating that sex stereotypes play a more consequential role for these candidates.

The quality of the challenger does not have a significant effect on vote decisions. For example, citizens are not more likely to vote for house members than for state legislators. While this is somewhat surprising given prior research (Abramowitz 1988; Jacobson 1987; Smith and Squire 1991; Squire 1989; Stewarts 1989), the nonfinding may be due to the small sample size. In this analysis we are analyzing citizens' reactions to only eighteen candidates.

Finally, most political pundits described 1992 as "the year of the woman." As indicated earlier, the impressive success of women candidates in 1992 cannot be attributed to the overabundance of "female" themes since these types of issues were not more prevalent in 1992 when compared to the two preceding election years. However, the impact of "female" themes may have been more powerful in 1992 than in earlier years. I test for this possibility by interacting campaign climate with the year of the election (1992 v. 1988 and 1990) in the OLS equation predicting evaluations of women candidates and in the logit equation predicting voting decisions. The results of the OLS regression indicate that the campaign climate was not more important in 1992 than in 1988 and 1990. The coefficient for the interaction term is -9.9 with a standard error of 7.0. Similarly, in terms of voting decisions, the impact of campaign climate was not more powerful in 1992 than in previous years. The coefficient for the interaction term in the logit equation is .92 with a standard error of .50.[16] Finally, when the analysis is restricted to nonincumbent races, we find similar results; the effect of the campaign climate is not conditioned by the year of the election.[17]

Given the persuasiveness of sex stereotypes and the responsiveness of political actors to the context of campaigns, certain campaign settings provide more opportunities for women candidates, just as other settings offer more obstacles. The interaction between people's beliefs about the capabilities and liabilities of women candidates and the setting of the campaign influences the electability of women candidates for statewide office.

In this chapter the survey data show that when the context of the campaign places a premium on women's stereotypical strengths, voters develop more favorable impressions of women candidates and are more likely to support these candidates at the polls. In contrast, when the salient themes in the campaign correspond to women's perceived weaknesses, the electoral prospects of women candidates are diminished. The relationship between the context of the campaign and people's views of women candidates is robust. Even after the traditional determinants of the vote are considered, the context of the campaign continues to be powerful, influencing overall evaluations of women candidates as well as intended vote choice.

The survey results described in this chapter, coupled with the theory and evidence presented in earlier chapters, provide insights regarding the unusual success of women candidates in 1992. Women made such impressive gains in 1992 because they were able to take advantage of the favorable electoral climate. Eleven women ran for the U.S. Senate in 1992. Of these eleven candidates, five were nominated to contest "winnable" seats; one candidate ran as an incumbent (Senator Barbara Mikulski), three competed in open seats (Barbara Boxer, Carol Mosley-Braun, Patty Murray), and one challenged (Diane Feinstein) an appointed incumbent. Each of these five candidates campaigned successfully for the U.S. Senate.

While "female" themes were also pervasive in 1988 and 1990, women did not have the opportunity to make substantial gains. In 1988 only two women ran for the U.S. Senate. In 1990 eight women campaigned for U.S. senator, but six of these eight candidates ran as challengers.[18] None of these challengers was successful in reaching the U.S. Senate. In 1992 three factors united to benefit women candidates uniquely: (1) the widespread adherence to sex stereotypes; (2) the prominence "female" themes; *and* (3) the significant number of women nominated to run in "winnable" races.[19]

Sex stereotypes are pervasive—they influence the behavior of candidates, reporters, and voters. In addition, since the consequences of sex stereotypes depend on the electoral climate, the electability of women candidates is contingent upon the campaign setting, with certain election years providing more opportunities for women candidates. The importance of stereotypes ties women's chances of election to the prevailing campaign climate. However, if stereotypes are reduced and preconceived notions about the typical liabilities and capabilities of women candidates are eliminated, then the press and voters will respond similarly to the campaigns of male and female candidates. Candidates will no longer need to consider people's stereotypical images when adopting campaign strategies. With the eradication of stereotypes, women's electoral prospects will no longer be contingent upon the campaign setting of the time and voters will consider the same criteria when evaluating men and women candidates.

10

Conclusions and Implications

✷

Women continue to be underrepresented in the U.S. political system. Although women participate in politics at least as much as men, women are not as likely to be elected to positions of power. This book finds that women's access to political office may be limited by people's stereotypical views of women's capabilities and liabilities. By influencing the behavior of candidates, the quality of press coverage, and the reactions of voters, these stereotypical views hamper women in their campaigns for higher political office. In this final chapter I review the major findings of this book. In addition, I describe how gender differences in news coverage influence people's interpretation of electoral mandates, and I offer advice on how women candidates may want to modify their campaign strategies as a way of circumventing stereotypes about their candidacies. I conclude by discussing how the pervasiveness of stereotypes affects the quality of political representation in the United States.

Summary of Results

In conducting campaigns for statewide office, candidates clearly consider people's stereotypical views of their candidacies when choosing between alternative campaign strategies. Women, who are viewed as more trustworthy spokespeople, are more likely to appear in their own ads. In addition, women respond to voters' doubts about their legitimacy by dressing professionally in almost all of their campaign advertisements. Similarly, women try to eradicate stereotypes regarding their competence and leadership ability by stressing these qualities in their campaign appeals more frequently than their male counterparts. By demonstrating their expertise and experience, women candidates hope to dispel doubts people have about their leadership ability.

Voters also consider the gender of the candidates when forming impressions of men and women candidates. These stereotypes are pervasive and consistently lead to more favorable views of women candidates. People see women as better able to deal with social issues such as education, health care, and women's issues, and women are considered more compassionate and more honest than equivalent male candidates. Furthermore, women are more likely than men to rely on stereotypes when drawing distinctions between candidates, suggesting that a candidate's sex is more salient to female voters. In addition, the frequency of stereotyping is negatively related to the amount of information available about the candidates. This indicates that stereotyping may be more common for candidates who receive less coverage, such as women candidates in senate contests.

Finally, the news media respond to the gender of the candidates when covering campaigns for statewide office. Women candidates in gubernatorial and senate campaigns consistently receive less issue coverage than their male counterparts. Instead, reporters prefer to emphasize the horse race when covering female senate candidates, providing voters with negative information about the viability of women candidates for the U.S. Senate. In gubernatorial contests reporters choose to concentrate on the personality characteristics of women candidates instead of on their issue concerns. This inequity in issue coverage, present in both senate and gubernatorial campaigns, is not driven by the campaigns of women candidates. In fact, the results of the political advertising analysis show that in their campaign appeals, women are just as likely as men to talk about their commitment to issues.

Overall, the press appears to be more responsive to the campaign messages of male candidates. In both gubernatorial and senate campaigns, men and women candidates choose to emphasize different policy concerns and personality characteristics. However, the correspondence between the news media's emphasis and the candidates' emphasis is consistently higher for male candidates in both gubernatorial and senate campaigns. The news media appear to echo the campaign messages of men candidates, while they largely distort the messages sent by women candidates.

Women may choose to stress different themes in their campaigns because they believe that these alternative strategies may be more effective for their unique candidacies. However, by potentially muting the campaign messages of women candidates, the news media hamper women in their electoral bids.

The media's misrepresentation of women candidates' campaign messages limits the effectiveness of women's campaigns.

While stereotypical views of men and women influence voters, candidates, and the press, the impact of these stereotypes on the electoral fortunes of women candidates depends on the campaign's context. When women's stereotypical strengths correspond to the salient themes of the campaign, women candidates have an advantage. On the other hand, when the important issues in the campaign highlight women's perceived weaknesses, women's electoral prospects are diminished.

First, the candidates consider the electoral environment when articulating a campaign agenda. In senate races, male candidates develop campaigns that emphasize the salient issues of the day (i.e., "male" issues), while female senate candidates try to alter the traditional agenda by focusing on "female" issues. In gubernatorial campaigns, where "female" issues are more prominent, male candidates respond by demonstrating their competence to deal with these "female" issues. Female gubernatorial candidates, in contrast, stress their commitment to "male" issues as a way of changing stereotypical views about their campaigns.

Second, the context of the campaign determines whether voters are likely to consider themes that highlight women candidates' traditional strengths rather than their traditional weaknesses. Finally, the news media respond to the context of the campaign by treating women candidates more equitably when there is a favorable correspondence between the campaign climate and people's stereotypical images.

Given the pervasiveness of sex stereotypes and the responsiveness of political actors to the context of the campaign, certain campaign settings provide more opportunities for women candidates than others. The examination of the NES/SES survey data, supplementing the experimental evidence, clearly indicates that when the context of the campaign places a premium on women's stereotypical strengths, voters view women candidates more favorably and are more willing to support these candidates at the polls. However, when the salient themes in a campaign highlight women's perceived weaknesses, support for women candidates declines significantly.

The Media-Determined Mandate

The findings described in this book demonstrate that gender differences in news coverage can influence the electability of women running for statewide office. Regardless of the electoral office, the media differentiate between men and women candidates and consistently do a better job representing the campaign messages of male candidates.

The news media not only influence how campaigns are contested, they also affect how victories are assessed. For instance, male candidates in U.S. Senate campaigns often articulate their commitment to economic problems, such as tax reform or balancing the budget. Furthermore, the news media routinely focus on these issues when covering campaigns, largely ignoring the social issues introduced by women candidates.

Given the public's reliance on the news media for information about the candidates, people following the senate campaign will become more concerned with these economic issues. Therefore, when journalists and the victorious senator interpret the meaning of the election, they are likely to conclude that the election signifies the public's concern with economic issues. This particular interpretation of the outcome is likely to affect the policy agenda adopted by government officials. If a winning candidate believes that the campaign's success rests on the public's commitment to the policy domains covered during the campaign (e.g., budget, tax policy), then this newly elected official is likely to spend time developing legislation in these areas. By highlighting the male candidates' agenda and affecting the public's priorities, the news media influence the direction of public policy following the election.

However, if the news media were to represent the priorities of women candidates at least as well as male candidates, it is likely that voters would see these alternative policy areas as important. In senate races, voters would become concerned with health and education issues and would develop more favorable views of women candidates, thereby promoting the election of women to public office. Furthermore, since voters would be more concerned with these alternative issues, the election of women to the Senate who endorse these policy initiatives might lead elected officials to see these alternative issues as important, leading senators to demonstrate their commitment to these areas of public policy.

Campaign Advice for Women Candidates

In developing campaign strategies, women candidates should think about the stereotypical images of their candidacies as well as about the campaign environment of the time. In addition, women candidates should consider the news media's treatment, since people's views of candidates are largely shaped by the news media. While political commercials offer voters some information about the candidates, this information will be more persuasive if it is reinforced by the news media.

According to this study, the media's coverage of campaigns may present an important obstacle for women candidates. First, the press spend less time describing the issue priorities of female candidates and more time discussing their viability and personality characteristics. Given that voters may be uncertain about the policy capabilities of women candidates, this consistent difference in issue coverage could lead voters to develop less favorable images of women candidates.

To combat this potentially damaging aspect of press coverage, women candidates should emphasize their policy concerns more frequently in their campaign appeals. While men and women currently spend about the same amount of time discussing issues in their electoral bids, this emphasis is not represented by the news media. To increase the news media's emphasis on their issue positions, women need to speak more extensively and persuasively about their policy concerns.

In addition, the news media are more responsive to the campaign agendas of male candidates than female candidates. Men talk about "male" issues in senate campaigns and "female" issues in gubernatorial campaigns, and the news media represent these issues in their coverage of the candidates. While men echo the salient issues of the campaign, women try to alter the prevailing agenda, especially in senate campaigns. The women candidates' strategy is largely ineffective, since the news media fail to represent this difference in emphasis.

Given the unresponsiveness of the news media, women candidates could be more effective if they adopt an alternative strategy in their electoral bids. In particular, women should demonstrate their commitment to the pervasive issues in the campaign instead of trying to change the agenda, since the latter strategy appears to be largely ineffective. When "female" issues dominate the electoral landscape, women candidates should take a cue from their male counterparts and stress these issues in their campaigns. Given the prevalence of "female" stereotypes, if "female" issues are especially prominent and stressed by both male and female candidates, women candidates are likely to be advantaged.

When "male" issues are particularly prominent, women candidates should demonstrate their concern for these issues in their campaigns. Instead of trying to alter the agenda by playing to their stereotypical strengths, as women did in senate races in the 1980s, women should demonstrate their competence in handling these "male" issues. Such a strategy is likely to lead to a greater correspondence between the news media's agenda and the female candidate's agenda and could lead to a more productive campaign strategy.

In addition, by demonstrating their competence in "male" issues at a time when these issues are salient to the public, women candidates may be able to eradicate potentially damaging sex stereotypes. If women persuasively argue that they can deal with issues such the economy as well as their male counterparts, then voters may revise their stereotypical views of men and women candidates.

Women incumbents can play an especially influential role in dispelling stereotypes, given the prominent press attention garnered by incumbent candidates. Since a few highly salient and critical instances can play "a dominant role in the disconfirmation" of stereotypes (Rothbart 1981), women incumbents can demonstrate their competence in dealing with "male" issues, thereby encouraging the revision and reduction of stereotypical views of women candidates. By providing people with information that disconfirms their stereotypical views, women incumbents can help to eliminate harmful stereotypes.

With regard to their emphasis on personality traits in their electoral bids, women candidates should continue their present strategy of stressing "male" traits in their campaign appeals. Unlike the situation regarding issue positions, the emphasis on traits is less responsive to changes in the context of the campaign. In particular, "male" traits such as competence and leadership receive substantial attention in races for governor and senator. Given the pervasiveness of these traits, women candidates need to demonstrate their possession of these "male" traits by stressing these characteristics in their appeals.

As with issues, women who stress these typically "male" traits in their campaigns will encourage voters to revise their stereotypical views of women candidates. Again, women incumbents can play a particularly influential role in modifying these stereotypes, since their candidacies will receive more extensive coverage in the news. For example, if people see a woman senator demonstrating her leadership ability during televised senate hearings, this disconfirming evidence is likely to alter people's preconceptions of the typical female senator.

In campaigns for statewide office, women candidates should stress "male" traits; they should also demonstrate their ability to deal with "male" issues when these issues dominate the electoral landscape. Such a strategy will lead to a reduction in the preconceptions about the strengths and weaknesses of women candidates, since voters and reporters will be exposed to candidates displaying behavior that conspicuously conflicts with their stereotypical beliefs. If notions about the typical liabilities and capabilities of women candidates are eliminated, then the press and voters will respond similarly to the campaigns of male and female candidates. Furthermore, with the elimination of sex stereotypes, women's electoral prospects will no longer hinge on the favorability of the campaign climate of the time.

Women's Election and the Quality of Representation

Given that stereotypes often work to limit women's access to positions of political power, what are the costs? What do we lose by underrepresenting women in government? First, the quality of representation in this country is likely to be hampered by the exclusion of women from positions of power. Men and women have different views toward policy, and these differences are not likely to be reflected in a male-dominated legislature. According to research initiated in the 1980s, men and women differ in their positions on issues, and these differences are consistent and robust (e.g., Schubert 1991; Shapiro and Mahajan 1986). For instance, women are less likely to endorse violent policy options, and women support capital punishment less often than men. Women are less likely to endorse military intervention in other countries, and they are more likely to favor strict gun control regulations. In addition, women are more likely to support "compassion" issues such as social welfare, education, health programs, and programs to assist the poor (e.g., Schubert 1991; Shapiro and Mahajan 1986).

If women are underrepresented in governing institutions, women's unique priorities could be ignored by male representatives who do not share their concerns. Carroll (1985) provides data suggesting that this may be the case: in 1970 a CBS News poll found that 78 percent of women favored the federal establishment of day care centers to oversee children of working women. However, more than twenty years later, a program offering quality child care has yet to be initiated by the federal government.

In addition to gender differences in the policy positions of the electorate, recent work suggests that women state legislators and women in the U.S. Congress have different agendas from their male counterparts (Dodson and Carroll 1991; Carroll, Dodson, and Mandel 1991; Kathlene, Clarke and Fox

1991; Poole and Zeigler 1985; Thomas 1991). This research shows that women have a distinctive impact on public policy; women legislators initiate legislation that is responsive to women's demands for equal rights and more reflective of women's policy concerns. For instance, results of a survey of men and women legislators in twelve state houses indicates that women are more likely to introduce legislation concerning rape, teen pregnancy, pay equity, day care, and domestic violence. In addition, women are more likely to work on legislation dealing with women's "traditional" areas of interest: health care, welfare of children, the elderly, housing, and education (Carroll, Dodson, and Mandel 1991).

These studies suggest that women legislators bring a unique perspective to government. Women legislators may endorse this alternative perspective because they hold the same policy views as women in the electorate. Or, women legislators may work on issues that concern women because they are more in touch with and more sensitive to women's perspectives on policy. Whatever the case, by limiting the number of women in elective office, we limit the attention of the government to predominantly male concerns and ignore the concerns of women and women legislators. A governing body that neglects a range of issues not only ignores the concerns of a large segment of the electorate but also may be less effective than a government addressing a wider spectrum of policy concerns.

In addition to differences in policy priorities, men's and women's traditional roles in society could influence how they govern. Several feminist theorists contend that women's experience as mothers produces women's greater sense of connection with others, their empathy, their nurturing capabilities, and their less decisive individuation (see Okin [1990] for a review). These qualities may lead women to adopt governing styles that are more cooperative, democratic, and inclusive than the governing styles employed by their male colleagues. In addition, women's nurturing role in society may influence their views of policy, leading them to emphasize government programs designed to help others (e.g., promoting quality health care, assistance for the poor).

However, women's unique perspective extends beyond their experience as primary caregivers. More generally, women hold different societal positions than men. For example, women's experiences in the workplace are fundamentally different from the experiences of men; women are likely to earn less money than men, they are more likely to work part-time, and they are more likely to work without health insurance. These (and other) differences in the positions of men and women are likely to influence women's perspectives on the government's role in society. Women, for instance, may be more likely to believe that government should ensure that all citizens have the following: access to adequate health care, an optional family leave policy at their place of employment, and protection from sexual harassment in the workplace. By underrepresenting women in government, we artificially narrow the government's views on policy and perhaps misrepresent the interests of women constituents.

Finally, since women do not hold positions of power in this country, women are led to believe that the political system is not open to them (Carroll 1994). While half of the citizens in this country are women, women still hold only a small minority of elected offices. Therefore, women could be more likely than men to question the quality of representation and the functioning of the U.S. system of government.

The present distribution of power in this country is likely to discourage women from participating in politics. While women currently vote as often as men in national elections, their attachment to the political system continues to lag behind their male counterparts. According to Gant and Luttbeg's (1991) examination of the 1988 election, women are less trustful than men and have lower levels of political efficacy. The greater level of alienation among women may stem from their view that the U.S. government is largely inaccessible to them.

If the closed nature of the U.S. electoral system promotes alienation among women citizens, then the current system could discourage extensive participation by women. Many skilled women, for example, may choose a career in the private sector, because they see a "glass ceiling" in government that hinders women's climb to positions of power. These women, who might make excellent leaders, stay away from government because their likelihood of success looks extremely limited. However, if more women were elected to visible leadership positions in this country, then people would see the system as more open. Women might then be encouraged to participate at greater levels. Making the government more inclusive and increasing women's involvement would ensure that the talents and skills of all citizens were fully utilized in governing the nation.

Notes

2. Stereotypes in Statewide Campaigns

1. Political commercials were unavailable for the other women senate candidates. In order to bolster the number of women candidates in the sample, I included New Jersey's 1982 senatorial candidate Millicent Fenwick in the sample. Fenwick was the only woman candidate in 1982 for whom advertisements were available.

2. See appendix 1 for a list of the candidates included in the political advertising sample. The political ads for this study were provided by the Political Commercial Archive at the University of Oklahoma.

3. See appendix 2 for a copy of the political advertisement code sheet.

4. I coded all commercials in the sample. To ensure the reliability of the coding, two checks were performed. First, I coded a sample of articles twice—once at the start of the coding process, and once near the end. This reliability check revealed that coding remained stable, with 98 percent agreement on most measures. Second, I assessed intercoder reliability. A coder unfamiliar with the objectives of the study coded a random sample of the political advertisements. The intercoder reliability agreement for this sample of ads was 96 percent, with agreement ranging from 100 percent for some coding categories to a minimum of 90 percent for other categories.

5. Only general election races between the two major party candidates have been included in the analysis.

6. For some race types, three races for each level of competitiveness did not exist. In these instances all available races were included.

7. This was not possible in the senate case since there were significantly more women senate candidates. Seventeen women ran for the U.S. Senate between 1984 and 1986 and nine of these women ran as challengers in noncompetitive races.

8. The largest circulating newspapers in Texas and Colorado could not be obtained; the state papers with the second largest circulation (the *Houston Post* and the *Denver Post*) were analyzed instead.

9. In races where the state primary was held after September 1, coding began the day after the primary.

10. See appendix 4 for a copy of the code sheet used in the content analysis of newspaper coverage. In conducting the content analysis, reliability checks were performed periodically. Reliability between the coders was high, averaging 92 percent agreement.

11. I do not examine the direct effect of political advertisements on voters' attitudes because more information about the candidates is provided via the news media than via political advertisements (Joslyn 1983). In addition, the news media's coverage of the candidate's campaign is likely to be more persuasive than the candidate's own communications because people view ads as propaganda, while they consider news reports to be more objective (Graber 1992).

3. Gender Differences in Campaign Appeals for the U.S. Senate

1. See chapter 2 for details about the sampling and analysis procedure.

2. In the analysis of political advertisements, I treat the candidate—not the ad—as the unit of analysis and weigh the ads accordingly. By using the candidate as the unit of analysis, I avoid giving more weight to candidates who have more ads.

3. This difference is statistically significant at p<.05. The p value is based on the difference in proportions test.

4. Wadsworth et al. (1987) conducted an experiment to see whether "aggressive ads" by female candidates produced more negative views of these candidates. Counter to their expectations, they found that the "aggressive ad" did produce more favorable views of the female candidate. The "aggressive ad," compared to the "nonaggressive ad," led undergraduates to view the woman candidate as more qualified, more experienced, and more effective. While the results of this experiment suggest that women may be viewed more favorably when they act unstereotypically, the internal validity of the experiment is somewhat limited since the two ads differed in ways other than the aggressive and nonaggressive nature of the advertisement.

5. This difference is statistically significant at p<.05. The p value is based on the difference in proportions test.

6. This difference is statistically significant at p<.01. The p value is based on the difference in proportions test.

7. This difference is statistically significant at p<.01. The p value is based on the difference in proportions test. We cannot examine whether women consider the gender of their opponent when choosing between negative and positive campaign strategies since currently few women run against other women.

8. This difference is statistically significant at p<.10. The p value is based on the difference in proportions test.

9. Of course, the agenda-setting role of political commercials will be most influential if the messages presented in the ads are reinforced by other sources of political communication such as the news media. I compare issue discussion in political ads to newspaper coverage later in this chapter.

10. I use the stereotyping literature to divide issues into "male" and "female" issues.

"Male" issues include those issues where men are considered more competent (e.g., foreign policy, defense, economics, and agriculture); "female" issues are those where women are considered more capable (e.g., minority rights, the environment, abortion, school prayer, drugs, and social programs).

11. As with issues, I use the sex-stereotyping literature to divide traits into "male" and "female" traits. "Male" traits are those traits that are seen as characteristic of men (e.g., strong leadership, knowledge, intelligence), while "female" traits are those that are consistently associated with women (e.g., warmth, compassion, honesty).

12. To examine the correspondence between what the news articles discuss and what the candidates feature in their advertisements, I restrict the following analysis to the thirty-two cases where both news content and political advertising data are available. With this sample of races, we can compare the candidate's discussion of policy and personal characteristics with the news media's coverage of these themes.

4. Differences in Campaign Coverage: An Examination of U.S. Senate Races

1. See chapter 2 for details about the sampling and analysis procedure.

2. Although measures of statistical significance are not entirely appropriate here because the present sample is not a random sample from a larger population (e.g., for female incumbents and female candidates in open races, the entire population has been included in the sample), statistical significance is reported in the tables because they may be helpful for interpreting the importance of the reported differences.

3. For the analysis stage of the research, races were initially divided into three levels of competitiveness based on (1) preelection ratings published in the *Congressional Quarterly* special election issue and (2) final vote returns. Because coverage patterns for competitive and somewhat competitive races are similar, these two categories of races are combined for analysis.

4. A newshole is a measure of the space available for news (i.e., not including advertisements) in newspapers.

5. Although these stereotypes about women may be based on experience, they are still considered stereotypes since individuals are systematically overgeneralizing from a few specific examples (Schneider, Hastorf, and Ellsworth 1979).

6. Female candidates in open races, on the other hand, are not disadvantaged by press assessments of viability. Unfortunately, since only a handful of female candidates run in open races, this instance of equitable press coverage is less consequential. Only three of the sixteen women running for the U.S. Senate between 1984 and 1986 were candidates in open races.

7. These gender differences in coverage of negative resources are statistically significant at p<.05. The p value is based on the difference in proportions test.

8. Although female incumbents, challengers, and open race candidates consistently receive less issue coverage than their male counterparts, these differences fail to reach statistically significance (p<.10). Again, with the small number of cases here, it is difficult to obtain statistically significant differences.

9. This difference is statistically significant at p<.05. The p value is based on the difference in proportions test.

10. The reporter's gender is not related to coverage of the horse race for male and female candidates.

5. The Impact of Coverage Differences and Sex Stereotypes in Senate Campaigns

1. Appendix 5 contains copies of the four prototype articles.

2. See appendix 6 for the exact wording of the senate questions.

3. The p value, or level of significance, is p<.01. The p value is based on the F statistic.

4. Each of these differences is statistically significant at p<.05. The p value is based on the F statistic.

5. Again, the reported differences are statistically significant at p<.05, based on the F statistic.

6. It is not clear why the female incumbent article produces more positive honesty assessments; honesty is not mentioned in either article. It may be that the female incumbent candidate's unconventional and independent issue priorities are responsible for the high honesty ratings.

7. The content analysis showed that on average twelve paragraphs are published each day about both male and female incumbents. In contrast, an average of eleven paragraphs is published each day for male challengers and an average of eight paragraphs is published for female challengers. These averages determined the length, in paragraphs, of each of the four prototype articles.

8. Sex stereotyping may be less frequent in the real political environment—compared to the experimental setting—because voters are exposed to more information about the senate candidates. It would be useful to explore sex stereotyping of senate candidates in the real political environment with national survey data. Unfortunately, the lack of information about candidate trait and issue assessments in national senate studies (e.g., the 1988–1992 National Election Study [NES]/Senate Election Study[SES]) makes this exploration impossible.

9. While this study shows that women endorse female stereotypes more often than men and that stereotyping along "male" dimensions is noticeably absent, these findings are not consistent with earlier studies (e.g., Rosenwasser and Dean 1989; Rosenwasser and Seale 1988; Sapiro 1981–1982). However, since the current inquiry is more recent and relies on a more representative nonstudent sample, I am confident of the validity of the findings. During this time period people's adherence to the feminist belief that "women's nurturance imbues their political orientations with a desire for peace, social welfare and tolerance" (Rinehart 1992:8) may have increased, leading people to view women candidates as uniquely qualified for dealing with certain issues as well as possessing specific personality characteristics. In addition, women may have been more likely than men to endorse these feminist beliefs, thus producing greater stereotyping along "female" dimensions for women respondents.

10. While differences in evaluations of the incumbents' honesty may be explained by coverage differences (see table 5.3) as well as by sex stereotyping, gender differences in ratings on education and women's issues are driven by sex stereotyping. Although respondents are given no information regarding the candidates' commitment to these issues, they believe that woman candidates can deal with these issues more effectively.

11. See table 5.2 for a description of the experimental conditions.

12. In statistical terms there is a two-way interaction between coverage and candidate gender $F(1,43)=3.00$, $p<.10$ for viability assessments.

13. In the U.S. Senate races of 1984 and 1986, eleven of the fifteen women candidates were challengers.

6. Differences in Campaign Appeals for Governor

1. See chapter 2 for details about the sampling procedure for the political advertising analysis.

2. This difference is statistically significant at $p<.01$. The p value is based on the difference in proportions test.

3. Like their counterparts in senate races (see chapter 3), male gubernatorial candidates are less likely to use attack ads when facing a female opponent. Male candidates for governor use negative advertisements 37 percent of the time when opposing a male candidate and 16 percent of the time when running against a woman. This difference is statistically significant at $p<.01$. (The p value is based on the difference in proportions test.)

4. In contrast to the majority of experimental findings, Ansolabehere, Iyengar, Simon, and Valentino (1994) do not find that negative advertising is counterproductive.

5. While variations in the campaign setting produce important differences in the style of advertisements employed by women candidates for governor and senator, the tactics utilized by these candidates also exhibit some similarities. These parallels persist because the impact of some stereotypes is not contingent upon the prevailing campaign setting. For instance, women candidates, regardless of the office they seek, are regarded as more trustworthy than men. Given people's beliefs about the superior integrity of women candidates, women gubernatorial candidates, like women candidates for U.S. senator, appear in their ads more frequently than their male counterparts. For example, women running for open gubernatorial seats are featured in virtually all of their ads (94%), while their male colleagues make appearances in only three-quarters of their commercials (78%). In addition, since voters are often skeptical about the qualifications of women candidates, irrespective of the electoral office they seek, women adopt strategies to assuage people's doubts. For example, women candidates dress in a professional manner in nearly all of their campaign commercials as a way of highlighting the legitimacy of their candidacies. In gubernatorial contests, women candidates are twice as likely (81% v. 40%) as their male candidates to select formal attire when appearing in their own commercials.

6. This difference is statistically significant at $p<.01$. The p value is based on the difference in proportions test.

7. This difference is statistically significant at p<.01. The p value is based on the difference in proportions test.

8. The difference between the women gubernatorial candidates' discussion of traits and the discussion of traits by the other types of candidates is statistically significant at the p<.05 level. The p value is based on the difference in proportions test.

9. The difference in the trait emphasis for male and female nonincumbents is statistically significant at the p<.01 level. The p value is based on the difference in proportions test.

10. To examine the correspondence between what the news articles discuss and what the candidates feature in their advertisements, I restrict the following analysis to the twenty-eight cases where both news content and political advertising data are available. With this sample of races, we can compare the candidate's discussion of policy and personal characteristics with the news media's coverage of these themes.

7. Press Coverage of Male and Female Candidates for Governor

1. See chapter 2 for details about the sampling and analysis procedure.

2. This difference is statistically significant at p<.10. The p value is based on the F statistic.

3. For instance, in competitive contests, the horse race is mentioned 17 percent of the time for male candidates and 15 percent of the time for female candidates.

4. Although the difference in viability assessments between male and female gubernatorial candidates (2.9 v. 2.7) is statistically significant, this difference is not very large in substantive terms.

5. The only exception to this pattern is among incumbents where male and female incumbents receive the same amount of coverage: 10 percent of the coverage of male incumbents discusses positive resources while 9 percent of the coverage of female incumbents mentions positive resources.

6. This difference is statistically significant at p<.01. The p value is based on the difference in proportions test.

7. This difference fails to reach statistical significance at p<.10. The p value is based on the T statistic.

8. This difference is statistically significant at p<.05. The p value is based on the T statistic.

9. This difference is statistically significant at p<.05. The p value is based on the difference in proportions test.

10. In chapter 6, I examined newspaper coverage for twenty-eight of the forty-two gubernatorial candidates. As note 10 in chapter 6 explains, the analysis in chapter 6 was restricted to the twenty-eight cases where both news content and political advertising data were available for the candidates.

11. These percentages are derived from data from figure 4.5 and table 7.1.

12. This analysis, based on the full sample of gubernatorial races, complements the findings presented in chapter 6. The difference between the candidates' messages and

news media coverage is statistically significant at p<.01. The p value is based on the difference in proportions test.

8. News Coverage and Gender in Gubernatorial Campaigns: An Experimental Study of the Female Candidate's Potential Advantage

1. I did not examine gender differences in coverage of open races in the senate experiment because open races with female senate candidates are relatively rare. Only 18 percent of the population of women senate candidates (1984–1988) competed for open seats. In gubernatorial elections, on the other hand, female candidates run for open seats more frequently. Between 1983 and 1988, 44 percent of the women candidates running for governor ran in open races.

2. Copies of the six prototype articles are displayed in appendix 7.

3. The randomization procedure was effective. The twelve experimental conditions were similarly constituted, on average, along the following demographic dimensions: age, education, race, and sex.

4. The same questionnaire was used in both the senate experiment and the gubernatorial experiment, with appropriate changes for office.

5. These differences are all statistically significant at p<.06. The p values are based on the F statistic.

6. Since both incumbent prototype articles describe the candidates as likely winners, the press assessments of the candidates' viability ared not directly responsible for differences in the respondents' electability ratings. Instead, overall differences in coverage patterns represented in the two prototype articles cause the differences in electability ratings.

7. As an example, the candidate in the female challenger article is described as "strong" because this trait, according to the content analysis, is often used by the press to describe female gubernatorial challengers. This characterization of the candidate as "strong" may lead people to consider the candidate as better able to deal with defense policy.

9. The Electoral Consequences of Stereotypes

1. While it may be informative to measure voters' reactions to female gubernatorial candidates, an appropriate dataset does not exist. The 1988–1982 Senate Election Study, for example, asks only a very limited set of questions about candidates running for governor.

2. The exact wording of the feeling thermometer question is: "I'll read the name of a person and I'd like you to rate that person using something called the feeling thermometer. You can choose any number between 0 and 100. The higher the number, the warmer or more favorable you feel toward the person; the lower the number, the colder or less favorable. You would rate the person at the 50 degree mark if you feel neither warm nor cold toward them. How would you rate (Senate Candidate's Name) using the feeling thermometer?"

3. The exact wording for the vote choice question is: "In the election for the United State Senate, the ballot listed: (Names and Parties of all U.S. Senate Candidates Listed on Ballot). Did you vote for a candidate for the U.S. Senate? [If yes], who did you vote for?"

4. I examined the relationship between feeling thermometer scores and vote choice by dichotomizing reported vote choice in the following categories: voting for woman candidate=1; voting for opponent =0; and nonvoters=missing. I employed logistic regression and regressed the feeling thermometer scores on the reported vote. The resulting coefficient was .03, with a standard error of .003 (p<.01), with the feeling thermometer scores predicting 80 percent of the cases correctly.

5. For the 1988 Hawaii race between Senator Spark M. Matsunaga and Maria Hustace, the *Congressional Quarterly* report contained no discussion of themes. Therefore, this race was dropped from the analysis.

6. Of course, the context of the campaign may be influenced by the gender of the candidate; certain issues may be more likely to surface in campaigns involving women candidates. While this may be the case, it is not a problem with the current analysis since I am controlling for the gender of the candidate by examining only people's reactions to women candidates.

7. A mean of .50 would have signified an equal number of "male" and "female" themes.

8. The mean difference in campaign themes for these two time periods is statistically significant at p<.05. The p value is based on the t statistic.

9. The exact question wording is: "Generally speaking, do you usually think of yourself as a Republican, Democrat, Independent, or something else?" If the respondent indicated Democrat or Republican, the following question was asked: "Would you call yourself a strong Democrat/Republican or a not very strong Democrat/Republican?" If the respondent did not indicate Democrat or Republican in response to the first question, the follow-up question asked: "Do you think of yourself as closer to the Republican party or to the Democratic party?" With these questions, I develop the standard seven-point scale.

10. The exact question wording is: "We hear a lot of talk these days about liberals and conservatives. Think about a ruler for measuring political views that people might hold, from liberal to conservative. On this ruler, which goes from one to seven, a measurement of seven would be very conservative. Just like a regular ruler, it has points in between at 2, 3, 4, 5, or 6. Where would you place yourself on this ruler, remembering that 1 is very liberal and 7 is very conservative, or haven't you thought much about this? Where would you place (Senate Candidate's Name) on this same scale where one means very liberal and seven means very conservative?"

11. Respondents who did not answer the ideological questions were recoded to middle of the scale.

12. The exact question wording is: "Was there anything in particular you like about (Senate Candidate's Name)?" Up to five responses were recorded. "Was there anything in particular that you didn't like about (Senate Candidate's Name)?" Up to five responses were recorded.

13. It is necessary to rely on the likes/dislikes question to measure traits since a close-ended trait measure is not included in the senate study. With the likes/dislikes measure, personality traits may look especially powerful since traits may be particularly salient to respondents who mention these characteristics in response to the open-ended questions.

14. Candidates may do better in campaigns highlighting "female" themes, not because they are women but because they are Democrats. Twelve out of the twenty-one women running for U.S. Senate between 1988 and 1992 were Democrats, and "female" themes often compliment the strengths of Democrats. I test for this rival hypothesis by adding two variables to the regression equation: an interaction term estimating the conditional relationship between the party identification of the candidate and the context of the campaign (party of candidate*campaign climate) and a variable measuring the party of the candidate. The results of this regression analysis show that the context of the campaign is not conditioned by the party of the candidate. The regression coefficient for the interaction term is -11.4 with a standard error of 7.0. The same pattern emerges when we examine only nonincumbent candidates. The regression coefficient for the interaction term is nonsignificant, -10.7 with a standard error of 7.0.

15. The presentation in table 9.2 is slightly different from the presentation in table 9.1. In particular, given the difficulty of interpreting the logit coefficient, I have included change in probability scores as a way of assessing the impact of each independent variable.

16. Neither the interaction coefficient in the OLS equation nor the interaction coefficient in the logit analysis is statistically significant at $p<.05$. However, in each case, the coefficient is in the predicted direction, suggesting the "female" themes may have been somewhat more influential in 1992.

17. The OLS interaction coefficient (year*campaign climate) predicting evaluations of nonincumbents is 12.3 with a standard error of 7.3. (n.s.) The logit interaction coefficient (year*climate) predicting voting decisions for nonincumbents is .77 with a standard error of .52 (n.s.). Again, each of the coefficients is in the predicted direction—although not statistically significant at conventional levels—suggesting that the impact of "female" themes may have been somewhat more powerful in 1992.

18. In 1990 Patricia Saiki of Hawaii ran against an appointed senator, Daniel Akaka.

19. Of course, women may have been successful in winning nominations for "winnable" seats because of the pervasiveness of "female" themes.

Appendixes

Sample of Political Advertisements

State and Year	Candidate	Office	Number of Ads
Arizona (1986)	Richard Kimball	U.S. Senate	4
Arizona (1986)	John McCain	U.S. Senate	14
California (1986)	Alan Cranston	U.S. Senate	12
Colorado (1984)	Nancy Dick	U.S. Senate	5
Colorado (1986)	Ken Kramer	U.S. Senate	15
Florida (1986)	Paula Hawkins	U.S. Senate	20
Illinois (1984)	Charles Percy	U.S. Senate	10
Illinois (1984)	Paul Simon	U.S. Senate	14
Illinois (1986)	Judy Koehler	U.S. Senate	4
Iowa (1984)	Roger Jepsen	U.S. Senate	10
Iowa (1984)	Tom Harkin	U.S. Senate	18
Maine (1984)	William Cohen	U.S. Senate	11
Maine (1984)	Elizabeth Mitchell	U.S. Senate	8
Maryland (1986)	Linda Chavez	U.S. Senate	8
Maryland (1986)	Barbara Mikulski	U.S. Senate	12
Massachusetts (1984)	John Kerry	U.S. Senate	9
Massachusetts (1984)	Raymond Shamie	U.S. Senate	8
Michigan (1984)	Carl Levin	U.S. Senate	10
Michigan (1984)	Jack Lousma	U.S. Senate	18
Minnesota (1984)	Rudy Boschwitz	U.S. Senate	14
Minnesota (1984)	Joan A. Growe	U.S. Senate	14
Missouri (1986)	Christopher Bond	U.S. Senate	22
Nevada (1986)	Harry Reid	U.S. Senate	19
Nevada (1986)	Jim Santini	U.S. Senate	19
New Hampshire (1984)	Gordon Humphrey	U.S. Senate	10
New Hampshire (1984)	Norman D'Amours	U.S. Senate	9

State and Year	Candidate	Office	Number of Ads
New Jersey (1982)	Millicent Fenwick	U.S. Senate	5
New Jersey (1982)	Frank Lautenberg	U.S. Senate	11
New Jersey (1984)	Bill Bradley	U.S. Senate	5
New Jersey (1984)	Mary Mochary	U.S. Senate	6
Oregon (1984)	Mark Hatfield	U.S. Senate	5
Oregon (1984)	Margie Hendriksen	U.S. Senate	5
Pennsylvania (1986)	Arlen Specter	U.S. Senate	3
Pennsylvania (1986)	Bob Edgar	U.S. Senate	13
Tennessee(1984)	Victor Asche	U.S. Senate	2
Tennessee(1984)	Albert Gore	U.S. Senate	2
Texas (1984)	Lloyd Doggett	U.S. Senate	7
Texas (1984)	Phil Gramm	U.S. Senate	7
California (1986)	George Deukkmejian	Governor	12
Connecticut (1986)	William A. O'Neill	Governor	8
Connecticut (1986)	Julie D. Belaga	Governor	14
Illinois (1986)	James Thompson	Governor	16
Illinois (1986)	Adlai Stevenson	Governor	3
Iowa (1986)	Terry Branstad	Governor	3
Iowa (1986)	Lowell L. Junkins	Governor	2
Massachusetts (1986)	Michael S. Dukakis	Governor	6
Massachusetts (1986)	George Kariotis	Governor	7
Nebraska (1986)	Helen Boosalis	Governor	14
Nebraska (1986)	Kay A. Orr	Governor	15
New Hampshire (1984)	John H. Sununu	Governor	6
New Hampshire (1988)	Paul McEachern	Governor	2
New Hampshire (1988)	Judd Gregg	Governor	12
Oregon (1986)	Neil Goldschmidt	Governor	19
Oregon (1986)	Norma Paulus	Governor	15
Pennsylvania (1986)	Bob Casey	Governor	17
Pennsylvania (1986)	William W. Scranton	Governor	24
Tennessee (1986)	Ned McWherter	Governor	16
Tennessee (1986)	Winfield Dunn	Governor	14
Texas (1986)	Mark White	Governor	10
Texas (1986)	Bill Clements	Governor	10
Vermont (1984)	Madeleine M. Kunin	Governor	6
Vermont (1984)	John J. Easton, Jr	Governor	6
Vermont (1986)	Madeleine M. Kunin	Governor	5
Vermont (1986)	Peter Smith	Governor	14
Vermont (1988)	Madeleine M. Kunin	Governor	6
Vermont (1988)	Michael Bernhardt	Governor	5

APPENDIX 2
Copy of Political Advertising Code Sheet

Variable Description	Code
Candidate Code	— —
Ad Number (Sequential)	— — —
Length of Ad (in seconds)	— — —

Type of Candidate	— —

1=Male Incumbent (v. Male Challenger)
2=Male Incumbent (v. Female Challenger)
3=Female Incumbent (v. Male Challenger)
4=Male in Open Race (v. Male)
5=Male in Open Race (v. Female)
6=Female in Open Race (v. Male)
7=Female in Open Race (v. Female)
8=Male Challenger (v. Male)
9=Male Challenger (v. Female)
10=Female Challenger (v. Male)

Type of Ad	— —

1=Positive Trait	6=Negative General
2=Positive Issue	7=Comparison
3=Negative Trait	8=Biography
4=Negative Issue	9=Endorsements
5=Positive General	10=Other

Candidate Dress	—

1=Informal Dress
2=Formal Dress
3=Both
0=Candidate not Pictured

Announcer	—

1=Male	2=Female

Actors in Ad	
Picture of Candidate	(1=Yes, 0=No)	—
Voice of Candidate	(1=Yes, 0=No)	—
Picture of Opponent	(1=Yes, 0=No)	—
Voice of Opponent	(1=Yes, 0=No)	—
Picture of Citizen	(1=Male, 2=Female)	—
Voice of Citizen	(1=Male, 2=Female)	—
Picture of Celebrity	(1=Male, 2=Female)	—

Voice of Celebrity	(1=Male, 2=Female)	___
Picture of Other Person	(1=Male, 2=Female)	___
Voice of Other Person	(1=Male, 2=Female)	___

Group References

Explicit   ___
     ___
     ___

Implicit   ___
     ___
     ___

Partisanship

Explicit   ___
Implicit   ___

Endorsements

Explicit

1=President	5=Celebrity	___
2=National Office Holder—Elective	6=Newspaper	___
3=National Office Holder-Appointive	7=Interest Group	___
4=State Office Holder	8=Former Office Holder	___
9=Other (Specify)		___

Implicit

1=President	5=Celebrity	
2=National Office Holder–Elective	6=Newspaper	___
3=National Office Holder–Appointive	7=Interest Group	___
4=State Office Holder	8=Former Office Holder	___
9=Other (Specify)		___

Criticisms of Opponent (number)   ___

Traits of Candidate (Number of Mentions)		Traits of Opponent (Number of Mentions)	
Honest	___ ___	Dishonest	___ ___
Trustworthy	___ ___	Untrustworthy	___ ___
Compassionate	___ ___	Weak	___ ___
Gentle	___ ___	Passive	___ ___
Intelligent	___ ___	Biased	___ ___
Analytical	___ ___	Emotional	___ ___
Effective	___ ___	Dependent	___ ___
Knowledgeable	___ ___	Uninformed	___ ___
Hardworking	___ ___	Erratic	___ ___
Tough	___ ___	Weak Leader	___ ___
Strong	___ ___	Ineffective	___ ___

Independent	__ __	Power-Hungry	__ __
Strong Leader	__ __	Immoral	__ __
Objective	__ __	Insensitive	__ __
Consistent, Stable	__ __	Inexperienced	__ __
Competitive	__ __	Other	__ __
Aggressive	__ __	Other	__ __
Experienced	__ __	Other	__ __
Other	__ __		
Other	__ __		
Other	__ __		

	Issues of Candidate (Number of Mentions)	Issues of Opponent (Number of Mentions)
Defense Issues	__ __	__ __
USSR/U.S. Relations	__ __	__ __
Central America	__ __	__ __
South Africa	__ __	__ __
Middle East	__ __	__ __
Europe	__ __	__ __
Foreign Affairs (General)	__ __	__ __
Economy (General)	__ __	__ __
Taxes	__ __	__ __
Budget/Govt. Spending	__ __	__ __
Energy/Oil Resources	__ __	__ __
Imports/Trade	__ __	__ __
Business	__ __	__ __
Farm	__ __	__ __
Fair Share for State (general)	__ __	__ __
Gay Rights	__ __	__ __
Environment	__ __	__ __
Abortion	__ __	__ __
Prayer in School	__ __	__ __
Drugs	__ __	__ __
AIDS	__ __	__ __
Health (other)	__ __	__ __
Women's Issues	__ __	__ __
Civil Rights/Race	__ __	__ __
Education	__ __	__ __
Employment/Jobs	__ __	__ __
Welfare	__ __	__ __
Care for Elderly	__ __	__ __
Other	__ __	__ __
Other	__ __	__ __

Open-Ended Description of Ad

APPENDIX 3
Sample of Races and Corresponding Newspapers for Content Analysis

Type of Race	State (Year)	Newspaper	Office
Male Incumbent v. Female Challenger	Colorado (1984)	*Denver Post*	U.S. Senator
Male Incumbent v. Female Challenger	Illinois (1986)	*Chicago Tribune*	U.S. Senator
Male Incumbent v. Female Challenger	Indiana (1986)	*Indianapolis Star*	U.S. Senator
Male Incumbent v. Female Challenger	Minnesota (1984)	*Minneapolis Star and Tribune*	U.S. Senator
Male Incumbent v. Female Challenger	Missouri (1982)	*Kansas City Times*	U.S. Senator
Male Incumbent v. Female Challenger	Nebraska (1984)	*Omaha World-Herald*	U.S. Senator
Female Incumbent v. Male Challenger	Florida (1986)	*Miami Herald*	U.S. Senator
Female Incumbent v. Male Challenger	Kansas (1984)	*Wichita Eagle-Beacon*	U.S. Senator
Female v. Male in an Open Race	Missouri (1986)	*St. Louis Post-Dispatch*	U.S. Senator
Female v. Male in an Open Race	New Jersey (1982)	*Newark Star-Ledger*	U.S. Senator
Female v. Female in an Open Race	Maryland (1986)	*Baltimore Sun*	U.S. Senator
Male Incumbent v. Male Challenger	California (1986)	*Los Angeles Times*	U.S. Senator
Male Incumbent v. Male Challenger	Illinois (1984)	*Chicago Tribune*	U.S. Senator
Male Incumbent v. Male Challenger	Iowa (1984)	*Des Moines Register*	U.S. Senator
Male Incumbent v. Male Challenger	Iowa (1986)	*Des Moines Register*	U.S. Senator
Male Incumbent v. Male Challenger	Michigan (1984)	*Detroit News*	U.S. Senator
Male Incumbent v. Male Challenger	New Hampshire (1984)	*Manchester Union Leader*	U.S. Senator
Male Incumbent v. Male Challenger	New Hampshire (1986)	*Manchester Union Leader*	U.S. Senator
Male Incumbent v. Male Challenger	Pennsylvania (1986)	*Philadelphia Inquirer*	U.S. Senator
Male Incumbent v. Male Challenger	Wyoming (1984)	*Casper Star-Tribune*	U.S. Senator
Male v. Male in an Open Race	Arizona (1986)	*Arizona Republic*	U.S. Senator
Male v. Male in an Open Race	Colorado (1986)	*Denver Post*	U.S. Senator
Male v. Male in an Open Race	Massachusetts (1984)	*Boston Globe*	U.S. Senator
Male v. Male in an Open Race	Nevada (1986)	Las Vegas Review Journal	U.S. Senator
Male v. Male in an Open Race	Tennessee (1984)	*Memphis Commercial Appeal*	U.S. Senator
Male v. Male in an Open Race	Texas (1984)	*Houston Post*	U.S. Senator
Male Incumbent v. Female Challenger	Connecticut (1986)	*Hartford Courant*	Governor
Male Incumbent v. Female Challenger	Missouri (1988)	*St. Louis Post-Dispatch*	Governor
Male Incumbent v. Female Challenger	Nevada (1986)	*Las Vegas Review Journal*	Governor
Female Incumbent v. Male Challenger	Vermont (1986)	*Burlington Free Press*	Governor
Female Incumbent v. Male Challenger	Vermont (1988)	*Burlington Free Press*	Governor
Female v. Male in an Open Race	Oregon (1986)	*Portland Oregonian*	Governor
Female v. Male in an Open Race	Kentucky (1983)	*Louisville Courier-Journal*	Governor
Female v. Male in an Open Race	Vermont (1984)	*Burlington Free Press*	Governor
Female v. Female in an Open Race	Nebraska (1986)	*Omaha World-Herald*	Governor
Male Incumbent v. Male Challenger	California (1986)	*Los Angeles Times*	Governor
Male Incumbent v. Male Challenger	Illinois (1986)	*Chicago Tribune*	Governor
Male Incumbent v. Male Challenger	Iowa (1986)	*Des Moines Register*	Governor
Male Incumbent v. Male Challenger	Massachusetts (1986)	*Boston Globe*	Governor

Male Incumbent v. Male Challenger	New Hampshire (1984)	*Manchester Union Leader*	Governor
Male Incumbent v. Male Challenger	New Jersey (1985)	*Newark Star Ledger*	Governor
Male Incumbent v.Male Challenger	Texas (1986)	*Houston Post*	Governor
Male v. Male in an Open Race	Colorado (1986)	*Denver Post*	Governor
Male v. Male in an Open Race	Maryland (1986)	*Baltimore Sun*	Governor
Male v. Male in an Open Race	New Hampshire (1988)	*Manchester Union Leader*	Governor
Male v. Male in an Open Race	Pennsylvania (1986)	*Philadelphia Inquirer*	Governor
Male v. Male in an Open Race	Tennessee (1986)	*Memphis Commercial Appeal*	Governor

APPENDIX 4
Copy of Code Sheet for Newspaper Content Analysis

Variable Description	Code
Newspaper Code	___ ___ ___
Date (Month/Day/Year)	___ ___ ___ ___ ___ ___
Article Number (Sequential)	___ ___ ___
Location of Article (Page Number)	___ ___ ___
Location of Article (Section)	___ ___
Length of Article (Number of Paragraphs)	___ ___ ___

Type of Article   ___

1=News Story	5=Magazine
2=Column	6=Letters to Editor
3=Editorial	7=Other (Specify)_____
4=News Analysis	_____

Sex of Author   ___

1=Male	3=Joint Authors (Male and Female)
2=Female	0=Cannot be ascertained

Type of Race   ___

1=Male Incumbent v. Male Challenger	5=Male v. Male in an Open Race
2=Male Incumbent v. Female Challenger	6=Male v. Female in an Open Race
3=Female Incumbent v. Male Challenger	7=Female v. Female in an Open Race
4=Female Incumbent v. Female Challenger	

	Candidate A (Incumbent/Winner-Open)	Candidate B (Challenger/Loser-Open)
Candidate Mentioned in Headline	___	___
1=Yes		
0=No		
Candidate Mentioned in Lead Sentence	___	___
1=Yes		
0=No		
Number of Paragraphs	___ ___ ___	___ ___ ___
Tone of Headline	___	___
1=Positive		
2=Negative		
3=Mixture		
4=Indifferent/Neutral		
0=Not about Candidate		

	Candidate A (Incumbent/Winner-Open)	Candidate B (Challenger/Loser-Open)
Tone of Article	___	___

    1=Positive   4=Indifferent/Neutral
    2=Negative   0=Not about Candidate
    3=Mixture

Candidate Criticized	___	___

    1=By Opponent   3=Unattributed
    2=By Other Source 0=Not Criticized

Horse Race Paragraphs	___ ___ ___	___ ___ ___

Horse Race Content (Polls, Debates)	___	___

    7=Likely Winner   3=Competitive, but Losing Ground
    6=Likely Winner, but Losing Ground 2=Noncompetitive, but Gaining Ground
    5=Competitive, but Gaining Ground   1=Noncompetitive, Sure Loser
    4=Competitive   0=No Mention of Horse Race

Endorsement in Newspaper	___	___

    1=Yes, Endorsement of Candidate
    0=No Endorsement Mentioned

Positive Campaign Resources	___	___

    1=Positive Resources Mentioned
    0=Positive Campaign Resources Not Mentioned

Negative Campaign Resources	___	___

    1=Negative Resources Mentioned
    0=Negative Campaign Resources Not Mentioned

Qualifications of Candidate		
1=Mention of Prior Elective Office	___	___
2=Mention of Prior Appointive Office	___	___
3=Mention of Other Qualifications	___	___
4=Mention of Lack of Qualifications	___	___

Traits (Number of Mentions)	Candidate A (Incumbent/Winner-Open)	Candidate B (Challenger/Loser-Open)
Honest	___ ___	___ ___
Trustworthy	___ ___	___ ___
Attractive	___ ___	___ ___
Compassionate	___ ___	___ ___
Gentle	___ ___	___ ___
Weak	___ ___	___ ___
Passive	___ ___	___ ___
Noncompetitive	___ ___	___ ___
Expressive	___ ___	___ ___
Biased	___ ___	___ ___
Emotional	___ ___	___ ___
Dependent	___ ___	___ ___
Unattractive	___ ___	___ ___
Uninformed	___ ___	___ ___
Erratic	___ ___	___ ___
Weak Leader	___ ___	___ ___
Unintelligent	___ ___	___ ___
Moral	___ ___	___ ___
Ineffective	___ ___	___ ___
Analytical	___ ___	___ ___
Effective	___ ___	___ ___
Knowledgeable	___ ___	___ ___
Hardworking	___ ___	___ ___
Tough	___ ___	___ ___
Strong	___ ___	___ ___
Vital	___ ___	___ ___
Intelligent	___ ___	___ ___
Independent	___ ___	___ ___
Strong Leader	___ ___	___ ___
Objective	___ ___	___ ___
Consistent, Stable	___ ___	___ ___
Competitive	___ ___	___ ___
Unexpressive	___ ___	___ ___
Ambitious, Power-Hungry	___ ___	___ ___
Immoral	___ ___	___ ___
Aggressive	___ ___	___ ___
Insensitive	___ ___	___ ___
Untrustworthy	___ ___	___ ___
Other _____	___ ___	___ ___
Other _____	___ ___	___ ___
Other _____	___ ___	___ ___

Issues (# of Paragraphs)	Candidate A (Incumbent/Winner-Open)	Candidate B (Challenger/Loser-Open)
Defense Issues	__ __	__ __
USSR/U.S. Relations	__ __	__ __
Nuclear Arms Control	__ __	__ __
Central America	__ __	__ __
South Africa	__ __	__ __
Middle East	__ __	__ __
Europe	__ __	__ __
Foreign Affairs (General)	__ __	__ __
Economy (General)	__ __	__ __
Taxes	__ __	__ __
Budget/Govt. Spending	__ __	__ __
Energy/Oil Resources	__ __	__ __
Imports/Trade	__ __	__ __
Business Regulation	__ __	__ __
Farm	__ __	__ __
Fair Share for State (General)	__ __	__ __
Gay Rights	__ __	__ __
Environment	__ __	__ __
Abortion	__ __	__ __
Prayer in School	__ __	__ __
Drugs	__ __	__ __
AIDS	__ __	__ __
Health (Other)	__ __	__ __
Women's Rights	__ __	__ __
Civil Rights/Race	__ __	__ __
Education	__ __	__ __
Employment/Jobs	__ __	__ __
Welfare	__ __	__ __
Care for Elderly	__ __	__ __
Other _____	__ __	__ __
Other _____	__ __	__ __
Other _____	__ __	__ __

Is Marital Status Mentioned?   __   __

1=Married   4=Widowed
2=Never Married   0=No Mention
3=Divorced, Separated

# of Paragraphs About Candidate's Spouse __ __   __ __

Are Children of Candidate Mentioned?   __   __

1=Yes
0=No

Is there a Picture of Candidate?   __   __

Male Incumbent Prototype Article
(With Male Candidate's Name)

Senator Parker Opens New Campaign Office
By John MacIntyre
(Page 12)

U.S. Sen. John Parker opened his new campaign headquarters in Phelps County today. A crowd was on hand to celebrate the opening and to wish Parker success in his bid for reelection.

After officially opening the new headquarters, Parker strolled through the streets of Carlisle, a nearby town, with his suit coat thrown over his shoulder. He stopped by Joe's Tavern for a cool drink and talked to some of the patrons.

In a speech delivered in Carlisle, Parker, the two-term senator and former lieutenant governor, stressed the importance of economic issues in the upcoming election. He explained that although the economy is strong nationally, economic prosperity has not been as great statewide.

Although his principal opponent in this year's senate race has said that Parker is insensitive to the needs of working people, Parker said Monday that he "will not rest until the people of this state are enjoying the economic prosperity that our friends in neighboring states have been enjoying." He said that further trade measures need to be implemented to help improve the economic situation here.

Besides stressing the need for tougher trade measures, Senator Parker also said that defense issues will play a critical role in the November elections. He said that he was encouraged by the progress made during the recent U.S.-Soviet summit meetings. He hoped that summit meetings between the two Superpowers would be continued by the next president.

Senator Parker does not face any tough competition in his bid for reelection. Polls show that he is far ahead of his principal opponents, and Senator Parker says that he is confident that he will be reelected.

In other political news, the three major television networks renewed their support for a national uniform poll-closing time on Thursday and promised in the meantime not to project a winner in any state in November's presidential election before polls closed in that state.

Representatives of ABC, CBS, and NBC told the Senate Rules Committee that they will make permanent their commitment to avoid early calling of state races if legislation is approved to have all polls in the continental United States close at 9 P.M. EST.

Steven Hessler of the Brookings Institute, a strong supporter of the senate legislation, attended the meeting. Thomas Ross, senior vice president for news at NBC, George Watson, vice president and Washington bureau chief of Capital Cities-ABC News, and Warren Mitofsky, vice president, election and survey unit, CBS News all expressed their committment to the senate legislation.

Hessler said that the networks had made the commitment previously, but that NBC had violated it during the New York Democratic presidential primary.

"I can assure you that was an inadvertant aberration and it will not occur again," NBC's Ross responded.

In 1984, Hessler said, all three networks had declared President Reagan's reelection by 5:30 P.M. EST.

Female Incumbent Prototype Article
(With Male Candidate's Name)

Senate Race May Turn Into Real Horse Race
By John MacIntyre
(Page 11)

Although recent polls show that this year's senate race will be a real horse race, U.S. Sen. John Parker is confident that he will be victorious in his reelection bid. At a press conference Monday, Parker said that he anticipates tough competition, but he said he believes that voters will send him back to the Senate.

Parker said that he has been an effective senator and that he has been successful in making changes in the Senate's legislative agenda. He cited the Child Abuse Reform Act as legislation that he has cosponsored. Parker said that "this legislation will be instrumental in securing funds to help detect potential victims of child abuse."

As well as cosponsoring the Child Abuse Reform Act, Sen. Parker said that he has been concerned about the drug problem for many years—long before it became a popular issue. He said, "Drug abuse is an important issue that transcends any particular election campaign."

Candidates should not offer "bandaids" to superficially fix the drug problem, Parker said. He said he hoped that intellectual and hard-hitting solutions would be offered and debated. His principal opponent in the senate race has said that Parker has failed to present any proposals of his own. Other critics agree by saying that Parker likes to talk about the problem of drugs but has yet to offer any legislation to deal with the problem.

Parker faces a tough reelection campaign. Although he has secured the endorsement of several consumer and environmental groups, polls show that this year's senate race will be close. Parker is running far behind his chief opponent in terms of campaign fundraising.

Polls show that Parker's support is strongest in the urban areas of the state. He needs to win these areas by large margins in order to counter his weak support in the outstate area.

In other political news, the three major television networks renewed their support for a national uniform poll-closing time on Thursday and promised in the meantime not to project a winner in any state in November's presidential election before polls closed in that state.

Representatives of ABC, CBS, and NBC told the Senate Rules Committee that they will make permanent their commitment to avoid early calling of state races if legislation is approved to have all polls in the continental United States close at 9 P.M. EST.

Steven Hessler of the Brookings Institute, a strong supporter of the senate legislation, attended the meeting. Thomas Ross, senior vice president for news at NBC, George Watson, vice president and Washington bureau chief of Capital Cities-ABC News, and Warren Mitofsky, vice president, election and survey unit, CBS News all expressed their committment to the senate legislation

Hessler said that the networks had made the commitment previously but that NBC had violated it during the New York Democratic presidential primary.

"I can assure you that was an inadvertant aberration and it will not occur again," NBC's Ross responded.

In 1984, Hessler said, all three networks had declared President Reagan's reelection by 5:30 P.M. EST.

Male Challenger Prototype Article
(With Male Candidate's Name)

Pols Predict Many Close Contests This Fall
By John MacIntyre
(Page 12)

Political experts through out the state are anticipating plenty of tight races this campaign season. Besides a close presidential race, this state's U.S. Senate contest is likely to be very competitive.

In the senate race here, Robert Dalton is trying to unseat Sen. Parker. Dalton is mounting a strong challenge according to recent polls, and the race is viewed as too close to call. Polls show that Dalton's support is greatest in the urban areas of the state and that he is gaining strength in the state's farming communities.

While some critics question his honesty, Dalton has stressed his leadership ability. If elected to the Senate, he said, he would emerge as a strong leader for the state.

Dalton has stressed the importance of the economy in the upcoming election. At at speech at the Rotary International Club luncheon Monday, Dalton said that although the economy is strong nationally, economic prosperity has not been as great here at home.

"I'm going to go to Washington and make things happen for the people of this state," Dalton told 125 people at the luncheon. "I will see to it that the people of this state take part in the nation's economic recovery."

Dalton also stressed the importance of tougher trade measures that would improve the economic situation here. He also said that defense issues would play a critical role in the November elections. Dalton said that he was encouraged by the progress made during the recent U.S.-Soviet summit meetings and he hoped that summit meetings between the two Superpowers would be continued by the next president.

In other political news, the three major television networks renewed their support for a national uniform poll-closing time on Thursday and promised in the meantime not to project a winner in any state in November's presidential election before polls closed in that state.

Representatives of ABC, CBS, and NBC told the Senate Rules Committee that they will make permanent their commitment to avoid early calling of state races if legislation is approved to have all polls in the continental United States close at 9 P.M. EST.

Steven Hessler of the Brookings Institute, a strong supporter of the senate legislation, attended the meeting. Thomas Ross, senior vice president for news at NBC, George Watson, vice president and Washington bureau chief of Capital Cities-ABC News, and Warren Mitofsky, vice president, election and survey unit, CBS News, all expressed their committment to the senate legislation.

Hessler said that the networks had made the commitment previously, but that NBC had violated it during the New York Democratic presidential primary.

"I can assure you that was an inadvertent aberration and it will not occur again," NBC's Ross responded.

Female Challenger Prototype Article
(With Male Candidate's Name)

U.S. Senate Candidate Robert Dalton Stresses Pocketbook Issues
By Jane MacIntyre
(Page 18)

The economy will play an important role in the elections this November, U.S. Senate candidate Robert Dalton said Monday. Dalton, speaking at the Rotary International Luncheon, said that although the economy is strong nationally, economic prosperity has not been as great statewide.

Dalton stressed the importance of tougher trade measures for improving the state's economic situation and said that stricter trade agreements would enhance the security of jobs here at home. He said that he believed the trade issue would play a critical role in the November elections.

Early polls showed Dalton far behind Sen. Parker but more recent polls indicate that Dalton may be gaining strength. A poll taken earlier this week by the *Observer* showed Dalton trailing the enator by 20 percentage points. A poll taken in February showed Dalton trailing the senator by more than 30 percentage points. The latest *Observer* poll also showed some gains for Dalton in terms of name recognition among statewide voters.

In terms of campaign finances, Dalton has failed to close the gap. Dalton is being outspent by a margin of 3 to 1. He has also failed to secure any significant support from Political Action Committees.

In other political news, the three major television networks renewed their support for a national uniform poll-closing time on Thursday and promised in the meantime not to project a winner in any state in November's presidential election before polls closed in that state.

Representatives of ABC, CBS, and NBC told the Senate Rules Committee that they will make permanent their committment to avoid early calling of state races if legislation is approved to have all polls in the continental United States close at 9 P.M. EST.

Steven Hessler of the Brookings Institute, a strong supporter of the senate legislation, attended the meetingThomas Ross, senior vice president for news at NBC, George Watson, vice president and Washington bureau chief of Capital Cities-ABC News, and Warren Mitofsky, vice president, election and survey unit, CBS News, all expressed their committment to the senate legislation.

In 1984, Hessler said, all three networks had declared President Reagan's reelection by 5:30 P.M. EST.

APPENDIX 6
Questions Assessing Attitudes Toward Senate Candidate

---

1. What is the likelihood that (John Parker) will win the election for U.S. Senate? Please circle the appropriate response.

     1. Very Likely   4. Not At All Likely

     2. Somewhat Likely   8. Don't Know

     3. Not Very Likely

2. Suppose the election were held today. What is the likelihood that you would vote for (John Parker) for U.S. Senate? Please circle the appropriate response.

     1. Very Likely   4. Not At All Likely

     2. Somewhat Likely   8. Don't Know

     3. Not Very Likely

3. You may have developed some mental image or picture of (Senator John Parker) as you read the article about him. There may be no particular reason for this image that you can think of, it may have just occurred to you as you read the article.

   What is your best guess about (John Parker's) competence in dealing with military issues? Please circle the appropriate response.

     1. Very Competent   5. Incompetent

     2. Competent   6. Very Incompetent

     3. Somewhat Competent   8. Don't Know

     4. Somewhat Incompetent

4. What is your best guess about (John Parker's) competence in maintaining honesty and integrity in government? Please circle the appropriate response.

     1. Very Competent   5. Incompetent

     2. Competent   6. Very Incompetent

     3. Somewhat Competent   8. Don't Know

     4. Somewhat Incompetent

5. What is your best guess about (John Parker's) competence for making decisions on farm issues? Please circle the appropriate response.

    1. Very Competent   5. Incompetent

    2. Competent   6. Very Incompetent

    3. Somewhat Competent   8. Don't Know

    4. Somewhat Incompetent

6. What is your best guess about (John Parker's) competence in improving the educational system? Please circle the appropriate response.

    1. Very Competent   5. Incompetent

    2. Competent   6. Very Incompetent

    3. Somewhat Competent   8. Don't Know

    4. Somewhat Incompetent

7. What is your best guess about (John Parker's) competence in dealing with health problems? Please circle the appropriate response.

    1. Very Competent   5. Incompetent

    2. Competent   6. Very Incompetent

    3. Somewhat Competent   8. Don't Know

    4. Somewhat Incompetent

8. What is your best guess about (John Parker's) competence in improving the economy? Please circle the appropriate response.

    1. Very Competent   5. Incompetent

    2. Competent   6. Very Incompetent

    3. Somewhat Competent   8. Don't Know

    4. Somewhat Incompetent

9. What is your best guess about (John Parker's) competence in dealing with the issue of women's rights? Please circle the appropriate response.

    1. Very Competent   5. Incompetent

    2. Competent   6. Very Incompetent

    3. Somewhat Competent   8. Don't Know

    4. Somewhat Incompetent

10. Think about (John Parker). The first phrase is "compassionate." In your opinion does the phrase "compassionate" describe (John Parker) *extremely well, quite well, not too well,* or *not well at all*? Please circle the appropriate response.

    1. Extremely Well   4. Not Well At All

    2. Quite Well   8. Don't Know

    3. Not Too Well

11. In your opinion does the phrase "provide strong leadership" describe (John Parker) *extremely well, quite well, not too well,* or *not well at all*? Please circle the appropriate response.

    1. Extremely Well   4. Not Well At All

    2. Quite Well   8. Don't Know

    3. Not Too Well

12. In your opinion does the phrase "honest" describe (John Parker) *extremely well,* quite well, *not too well,* or *not well at all*? Please circle the appropriate response.

    1. Extremely Well   4. Not Well At All

    2. Quite Well   8. Don't Know

    3. Not Too Well

13.   In your opinion does the phrase "knowledgeable" describe (John Parker) *extremely well, quite well, not too well,* or *not well at all*? Please circle the appropriate response.

    1. Extremely Well   4. Not Well At All

    2. Quite Well   8. Don't Know

    3. Not Too Well

Prototype Articles Used in Gubnernatorial Experiment

Male Incumbent Prototype Article
(With Male Candidate's Name)

Thompkins Addresses Lion's Club
By Paul Dusik
(Page 10)

Gov. Robert Thompkins discussed his bid for reelection during a luncheon for the Hampton Lion's Club yesterday.

Thompkins said that he thinks the top issue facing the state is the quality of the public education system at both elementary and secondary levels.

"Education is crucial," said Thompkins who is on a 15-day statewide campaign trip. Hampton is the third city on his agenda.

Thompkins also said something must be done about the state's "skyrocketing taxes." The average person cannot afford these kinds of increases, he said.

However, Thompkins's policy ideas have recently come under fire by senate leader Thomas McMann who called Thompkins's policies shortsighted and the chairman of the Joint Legislative Budget Committee who called them economically unsound.

Thompkins does not face any tough competition in his bid for reelection. Polls show that he is more than 20 percentage points ahead of his closest opponent.

And earlier this week Thompkins secured the much sought after endorsement of the AAFC.

In other political news, senate Democrats bluntly told the Bush administration yesterday that Congress will not permit oil exploration in the Arctic National Wildlife Refuge unless the administration accepts some increase in mandatory auto mileage efficiency standards.

Firing the first shots in what promises to be a tough battle over energy and environment policy, key senate Democrats told Energy Secretary James D. Watkins that the national energy strategy proposed by President Bush on Wednesday will not be accepted because it is not strong enough on energy conservation.

Bush's energy plan is a complex, 214-page document that covers all aspects of energy use and regulation, but the senators made clear that the political debate will focus on their demands for one basic tradeoff: If they are going to grant the administration's request to allow oil exploration in the ecologically sensitive wildlife preserve on Alaska's north slope, they are going to offer environmental groups an increase in the federal Corporate Average Fuel Economy rules, known as CAFE standards.

"If anybody thinks we're going to have a revolutionary energy strategy based only on more production, he's dead wrong," said Sen. J. Bennett Johnston (D-La.), chairman of the Senate Energy and Natural Resources Committee. "Congress won't pass it." But if Congress approves legislation based only on mandatory conservation, he said, President Bush will veto it.

Such an impasse, he said, "is not in the national interest."

Sens. Dale Bumpers (Ark.), Lloyd Bentsen (Tex.), Timothy E. Wirth (Colo.), and several other key Democrats said they could not accept the Bush plan without greater emphasis on energy conservation and environmental protection.

Under current law, each automaker's range of models is required to have an average mileage rating of 27.5 miles per gallon of gasoline. A bill sponsored by Sens. Richard H. Bryan (D-Nev.) and Slade Gorton (R-Wash.) would raise the requirement to about 40 miles a gallon by 2001.

Female Incumbent Prototype Article
(With Male Candidate's Name)

Lion's Club Members Weigh Candidate Issue Positions
By Paul Dusik
(Page 5)

The Hampton Lion's Club is weighing its options in deciding who to endorse as its candidate for governor.

Yesterday morning members heard from Gov. Vince Simpson who is the front-runner in recent polls and considered a "likely winner" by political analysts. Simpson's strength also rests with the fact that he has raised nearly twice as much in campaign monies as his top challenger.

Simpson said that he thinks the top issue facing the state is the quality of the public education system at both elementary and secondary levels.

Simpson also said something must be done about the state's "skyrocketing taxes." The average person cannot afford these kinds of increases, he said.

However, the governor's policy ideas have recently come under fire by senate leader Thomas McMann who called Simpson's policies economically unsound. He has also been criticized by House leaders who called him untrustworthy.

In other political news, senate Democrats bluntly told the Bush administration yesterday that Congress will not permit oil exploration in the Arctic National Wildlife Refuge unless the administration accepts some increase in mandatory auto mileage efficiency standards.

Firing the first shots in what promises to be a tough battle over energy and environment policy, key senate Democrats told Energy Secretary James D. Watkins that the national energy strategy proposed by President Bush on Wednesday will not be accepted because it is not strong enough on energy conservation.

Bush's energy plan is a complex, 214-page document that covers all aspects of energy use and regulation, but the senators made clear that the political debate will focus on their demands for one basic tradeoff: If they are going to grant the administration's request to allow oil exploration in the ecologically sensitive wildlife preserve on Alaska's north slope, they are going to offer environmental groups an increase in the federal Corporate Average Fuel Economy rules, known as CAFE standards.

"If anybody thinks we're going to have a revolutionary energy strategy based only on more production, he's dead wrong," said Sen. J. Bennett Johnston (D-La.), chairman of the Senate Energy and Natural Resources Committee. "Congress won't pass it." But if Congress approves legislation based only on mandatory conservation, he said, President Bush will veto it.

Such an impasse, he said, "is not in the national interest."

Sens. Dale Bumpers (Ark.), Lloyd Bentsen (Tex.), Timothy E. Wirth (Colo.) and several other key Democrats said they could not accept the Bush plan without greater emphasis on energy conservation and environmental protection, such as tighter CAFE standards.

Male Challenger Prototype Article
(With Male Candidate's Name)

Lion's Club Members Weigh Candidate Issue Positions
By Paul Dusik
(Page 10)

The Hampton Lion's Club is weighing its options in deciding who to endorse as its candidate for governor.

Yesterday morning members heard from gubernatorial candidate Michael Kern who is trailing in recent polls and considered a "long shot" by political analysts. Although the flow of campaign resources for Kern has been sporadic, his campaign has recently seen a significant rise in contributions.

Kern said that he thinks the top issue facing the state is the quality of the public education system at both elementary and secondary levels.

Kern also said something must be done about the state's "skyrocketing taxes." The average person cannot afford these kinds of increases, he said.

However, the candidate's policy ideas have recently come under fire by senate leader Thomas McMann who called Kern's policies shortsighted.

In other political news, senate Democrats bluntly told the Bush administration yesterday that Congress will not permit oil exploration in the Arctic National Wildlife Refuge unless the administration accepts some increase in mandatory auto mileage efficiency standards.

Firing the first shots in what promises to be a tough battle over energy and environment policy, key senate Democrats told Energy Secretary James D. Watkins that the national energy strategy proposed by President Bush on Wednesday will not be accepted because it is not strong enough on energy conservation.

Bush's energy plan is a complex, 214-page document that covers all aspects of energy use and regulation, but the senators made clear that the political debate will focus on their demands for one basic tradeoff: If they are going to grant the administration's request to allow oil exploration in the ecologically sensitive wildlife preserve on Alaska's north slope, they are going to offer environmental groups an increase in the federal Corporate Average Fuel Economy rules, CAFE standards.

"If anybody thinks we're going to have a revolutionary energy strategy based only on more production, he's dead wrong," said Sen. J. Bennett Johnston (D-La.), chairman of the Senate Energy and Natural Resources Committee. "Congress won't pass it." But if Congress approves legislation based only on mandatory conservation, he said, President Bush will veto it.

Such an impasse, he said, "is not in the national interest."

Sens. Dale Bumpers (Ark.), Lloyd Bentsen (Tex.), Timothy E. Wirth (Colo.) and several other key Democrats said they could not accept the Bush plan without greater emphasis on energy conservation and environmental protection, such as tighter CAFE standards.

Under current law, each automaker's range of models is required to have an average mileage rating of 27.5 miles per gallon of gasoline. A bill sponsored by Sens. Richard H. Bryan (D-Nev.) and Slade Gorton (R-Wash.) would raise the requirement to about 40 miles a gallon by 2001.

Most environmental groups support the bill, saying it would save the country about 2.8 million barrels of oil a day when fully effective. The United States consumes about 17 million barrels a day. But the Bush administration opposes higher standards on several grounds, contending they would save less oil than projected and require the production of smaller cars that would be unsafe.

Female Challenger Prototype Article
(With Male Candidate's Name)

Lion's Club Members Weigh Candidate Issue Positions
   By Paul Dusik
   (Page 5)

The Hampton Lion's Club is weighing its options in deciding who to endorse as its candidate for governor.

Yesterday morning members heard from gubernatorial candidate Samuel Byer who is finishing up his 15-day statewide campaign trip.

Byer said that he thinks the top issues facing the state are the quality of the public education system and "skyrocketing taxes."

However, the candidate's policy ideas have recently come under fire by senate leader Thomas McMann who called Byer's policies shortsighted. And while Byer has a highly qualified campaign staff working on his behalf, campaign funding has been slow.

Byer, who has been referred to as strong by House leaders, continues to be a viable candidate in this race and, although behind in the polls, is within striking distance of the leaders.

In other political news, senate Democrats bluntly told the Bush administration yesterday that Congress will not permit oil exploration in the Arctic National Wildlife Refuge unless the administration accepts some increase in mandatory auto mileage efficiency standards.

Firing the first shots in what promises to be a tough battle over energy and environment policy, key senate Democrats told Energy Secretary James D. Watkins that the national Energy Strategy proposed by President Bush on Wednesday will not be accepted because it is not strong enough on energy conservation.

Bush's energy plan is a complex, 214-page document that covers all aspects of energy use and regulation, but the senators made clear that the political debate will focus on their demands for one basic tradeoff: If they are going to grant the administration's request to allow oil exploration in the ecologically sensitive wildlife preserve on Alaska's north slope, they are going to offer environmental groups an increase in the federal Corporate Average Fuel Economy rules, known as CAFE standards.

"If anybody thinks we're going to have a revolutionary energy strategy based only on more production, he's dead wrong," said Sen. J. Bennett Johnston (D-La.), chairman of the Senate Energy and Natural Resources Committee. "Congress won't pass it." But if Congress approves legislation based only on mandatory conservation, he said, President Bush will veto it.

Such an impasse, he said, "is not in the national interest."

Sens. Dale Bumpers (Ark.), Lloyd Bentsen (Tex.), Timothy E. Wirth (Colo.) and several other key Democrats said they could not accept the Bush plan without greater emphasis on energy conservation and environmental protection, such as tighter CAFE standards.

Under current law, each automaker's range of models is required to have an average mileage rating of 27.5 miles per gallon of gasoline. A bill sponsored by Sens. Richard H. Bryan (D-Nev.) and Slade Gorton (R-Wash.) would raise the requirement to about 40 miles a gallon by 2001.

Most environmental groups support the bill, saying it would save the country about 2.8 million barrels of oil a day when fully effective. The United States consumes about 17 million barrels a day. But the Bush administration opposes higher standards on several grounds, contending they would save less oil than projected and require the production of smaller cars that would be unsafe.

Watkins, referring to the CAFE bill as "the highway death act of 1991," said that "even if we could average 40 miles per gallon for new cars in the year 2000, the oil savings in 2005 would be 500,000 barrels a day," not 2.8 million. Provisions of the Bush energy plan that would require owners of fleets of vehicles to begin using fuels other than gasoline by 1995 would save 1.5 million barrels of oil a day, he said.

Prototype Article for Male Candidate in Open Race
(With Male Candidate's Name)

Finney Addresses Lion's Club
By Paul Dusik
(Page 8)

Gubernatorial candidate Scott Finney discussed his campaign during a luncheon for the Hampton Lion's Club yesterday.

Finney said that he thinks the top issue facing the state is the quality of the public education system at both elementary and secondary levels.

The candidate also said something must be done about the state's "skyrocketing taxes." The average person cannot afford these kinds of increases, Finney said.

However, Finney's policy ideas have recently come under fire by senate leader Thomas McMann who called his policies shortsighted and the chairman of the Joint Legislative Budget Committee who called them economically unsound.

Finney, who, according to recent polls, is running neck-and-neck with his challengers, was complemented for his strong leadership skills by House Speaker Joe Stiles.

And earlier this week, Finney secured the endorsement of the AAFC.

In other political news, senate Democrats bluntly told the Bush administration yesterday that Congress will not permit oil exploration in the Arctic National Wildlife Refuge unless the administration accepts some increase in mandatory auto mileage efficiency standards.

Firing the first shots in what promises to be a tough battle over energy and environment policy, key senate Democrats told Energy Secretary James D. Watkins that the national energy strategy proposed by President Bush on Wednesday will not be accepted because it is not strong enough on energy conservation.

Bush's energy plan is a complex, 214-page document that covers all aspects of energy use and regulation, but the senators made clear that the political debate will focus on their demands for one basic tradeoff: If they are going to grant the administration's request to allow oil exploration in the ecologically sensitive wildlife preserve on Alaska's north slope, they are going to offer environmental groups an increase in the federal Corporate Average Fuel Economy rules, known as CAFE standards.

"If anybody thinks we're going to have a revolutionary energy strategy based only on more production, he's dead wrong," said Sen. J. Bennett Johnston (D-La.), chairman of the Senate Energy and Natural Resources Committee. "Congress won't pass it." But if Congress approves legislation based only on mandatory conservation, he said, President Bush will veto it.

Such an impasse, he said, "is not in the national interest."

Sens. Dale Bumpers (Ark.), Lloyd Bentsen (Tex.), Timothy E. Wirth (Colo.) and several other key Democrats said they could not accept the Bush plan without greater emphasis on energy conservation and environmental protection, such as tighter CAFE standards.

Under current law, each automaker's range of models is required to have an average mileage rating of 27.5 miles per gallon of gasoline. A bill sponsored by Sens. Richard H. Bryan (D-Nev.) and Slade Gorton (R-Wash.) would raise the requirement to about 40 miles a gallon by 2001.

Most environmental groups support the bill, saying it would save the country about 2.8 million barrels of oil a day when fully effective. The United States consumes about 17 million barrels a day. But the Bush administration opposes higher standards on several grounds, contending they would save less oil than projected and require the production of smaller cars that would be unsafe.

Watkins, referring to the CAFE bill as "the highway death act of 1991," said that "even if we could average 40 miles per gallon for new cars in the year 2000, the oil savings in 2005 would be 500,000 barrels a day," not 2.8 million. Provisions of the Bush energy plan that would require owners of fleets of vehicles to begin using fuels other than gasoline by 1995 would save 1.5 million barrels of oil a day, he said.

Johnston and Sen. Malcolm Wallop (R-Wyo.) have introduced a comprehensive energy bill and plan to use it, rather than the Bush proposal, as the vehicle for congressional action on energy issues this year. It would include an increase in CAFE standards, but would set no specific mileage objective until the Transportation Department had studied the likely composition of the nation's future vehicle fleet.

Prototype Article for Female Candidate in Open Race
(With Male Candidate's Name)

Howe Addresses Lion's Club
    By Paul Dusik
    (Page 10)

Gubernatorial candidate Larry Howe discussed his campaign during a luncheon for the Hampton Lion's Club yesterday.

Howe told the group of 200 members that he thinks something must be done about the state's "skyrocketing taxes."

The average person cannot afford these kinds of increases, he said. He recommended restructuring the tax system and pledged to eliminate unfair tax burdens.

Howe, who has been called a "strong leader" by House Speaker Joe Stiles, continues to be a viable candidate in this race and, although behind in the polls, is within striking distance of the leaders.

His exceptional fund-raising abilities have given him a jump in the field in the area of campaign resources.

Howe, who is finishing up a 15-day statewide fund-raising bout, has raised nearly $400,000 more than any other candidate.

However, Howe's policy ideas have recently come under fire by senate leader Thomas McMann who called his policies short-sighted and economically unsound.

In other political news, senate Democrats bluntly told the Bush administration yesterday that Congress will not permit oil exploration in the Arctic National Wildlife Refuge unless the administration accepts some increase in mandatory auto mileage efficiency standards.

Firing the first shots in what promises to be a tough battle over energy and environment policy, key senate Democrats told Energy Secretary James D. Watkins that the national energy strategy proposed by President Bush on Wednesday will not be accepted because it is not strong enough on energy conservation.

Bush's energy plan is a complex, 214-page document that covers all aspects of energy use and regulation, but the senators made clear that the political debate will focus on their demands for one basic tradeoff: If they are going to grant the administration's request to allow oil exploration in the ecologically sensitive wildlife preserve on Alaska's north slope, they are going to offer environmental groups an increase in the federal Corporate Average Fuel Economy rules, known as CAFE standards.

"If anybody thinks we're going to have a revolutionary energy strategy based only on more production, he's dead wrong," said Sen. J. Bennett Johnston (D-La.), chairman of the Senate Energy and Natural Resources Committee. "Congress won't pass it." But if Congress approves legislation based only on mandatory conservation, he said, President Bush will veto it.

Such an impasse, he said, "is not in the national interest."

Sens. Dale Bumpers (Ark.), Lloyd Bentsen (Tex.), Timothy E. Wirth (Colo.) and several other key Democrats said they could not accept the Bush plan without greater emphasis on energy conservation and environmental protection, such as tighter CAFE standards.

Under current law, each automaker's range of models is required to have an average mileage rating of 27.5 miles per gallon of gasoline. A bill sponsored by Sens. Richard H. Bryan (D-Nev.) and Slade Gorton (R-Wash.) would raise the requirement to about 40 miles a gallon by 2001.

Most environmental groups support the bill, saying it would save the country about 2.8 million barrels of oil a day when fully effective. The United States consumes about 17 million barrels a day. But the Bush administration opposes higher standards on several grounds, contending they would save less oil than projected and require the production of smaller cars that would be unsafe.

Watkins, referring to the CAFE bill as "the highway death act of 1991," said that "even if we could average 40 miles per gallon for new cars in the year 2000, the oil savings in 2005 would be 500,000 barrels a day," not 2.8 million. Provisions of the Bush energy plan that would require owners of fleets of vehicles to begin using fuels other than gasoline by 1995 would save 1.5 million barrels of oil a day, he said.

Bibliography

Ansolabehere, Steven, Roy Behr, and Shanto Iyengar. 1993. *The Media Game: American Politics in the Television Age.* New York: Macmillan.

Ansolabehere, Steven and Shanto Iyengar. 1991. "Why Candidates Attack: Effects of Television Advertising in the 1990 California Gubernatorial Campaign." Presented at the annual meeting of the Western Political Science Association, Seattle.

Ashmore, Richard D. and Frances K. Del Boca. 1979. "Sex Stereotypes and Implicit Personality Theory: Towards a Cognitive-Social Psychological Conceptualization." *Sex Roles* 5:219–248.

Ashmore, Richard D., Frances K. Del Boca, and Arthur J. Wohlers. 1986. "Gender Stereotypes." In *The Social Psychology of Female-Male Relations: A Critical Analysis of Central Concepts*, ed. Richard D. Ashmore and Frances K. Del Boca. Orlando, Fla: Academic Press.

Bem, Sandra. 1981. "Gender Schema Theory: A Cognitive Account of Sex Typing." *Psychological Review* 88:354–364.

Benze, J. G. and E. R. Declerq. 1985. "Content of Television Political Ads for Female Candidates. *Journalism Quarterly* 62:278–283, 288.

Broverman, Inge, Susan R. Vogel, Donald M. Broverman, Frank E. Clarkson, and Paul S. Rosenkrantz. 1974. "Sex Role Stereotypes: A Current Appraisal." *Journal of Social Issues* 28:59–78.

Carroll, Susan. 1985. *Women as Candidates in American Politics.* Bloomington: Indiana University Press.

Carroll, Susan. 1994. *Women as Candidates in American Politics.* Bloomington: Indiana University Press.

Carroll, Susan, Debra L. Dodson, and Ruth B. Mandel. 1991. "The Impact of Women in Public Office: An Overview." Center for the American Woman and Politics (CAWP) Fact Sheet. 1993. Rutgers N.J.: Eagleton Institute of Politics, Rutgers University.

Darcy, R., Susan Welch, and Janet Clark. 1987. *Women, Elections, and Representation*. New York: Longman.

Deaux, Kay and Laurie L. Lewis. 1984. "Structure of Gender Stereotypes: Interrelationships Among Components and Gender Label." *Journal of Personality and Social Psychology* 46:991–1004.

Deber, Raisa B. 1982. " 'The Fault, Dear Brutus': Women as Congressional Candidates in Pennsylvania." *Journal of Politics* 144:463–479.

Dodson, Debra L. and Susan J. Carroll. 1991. *Reshaping the Agenda: Women in State Legislatures*. Rutgers N.J.: Center for the American Woman and Politics, Eagleton Institute of Politics, Rutgers University.

Ekstrand, L. E. and W. Eckert. 1981. "The Impact of Candidate's Sex on Voter Choice." *Western Political Quarterly* 34:78–87.

Epstein, Edward Jay. 1973. *News From Nowhere*. New York: Vintage.

Erbring, Lutz E., Edie N. Goldenberg, and Arthur H. Miller. 1980. "Front-Page News and Real World Cues: A New Look at Agenda-Setting by the Media." *American Journal of Political Science* 24:16–49.

Feather, N. T. and J. G. Simon. 1975. "Reactions to Male and Female Success in Sex-Linked Occupations: Impressions of Personality, Causal Attribution, and Perceived Likelihood of Different Consequences." *Journal of Personality and Social Psychology* 31:20–31.

Ferejohn, John A. 1977. "On the Decline of Competition in Congressional Elections." *American Political Science Review* 71:166–176.

Fiorina, Morris P. 1977. *Congress: The Keystone of the Washington Establishment*. New Haven: Yale University Press.

Fiske, Susan R. and Steven L. Neuberg. 1990. "A Continuum of Impression Formation From Category-Based to Individuating Processes: Influences of Information and Motivation on Attention and Interpretation." In *Advances in Experimental Social Psychology*. Vol. 23, ed. Mark P. Zanna. San Diego: Academic Press.

Fiske, Susan T., Steven L. Neuberg, Ann E. Beattie, and Sandra J. Milberg. 1987. "Category-Based and Attribute-Based Reactions to Others: Some Informational Conditions of Stereotyping and Individuating Processes." *Journal of Experimental Social Psychology* 23:399–427.

Gallup Report. 1984. Vol. 228:2–14.

Gant, Michael and Norman R Luttbeg. 1991. *American Electoral Behavior: 1952–1988*. Itasca, Ill.: F. E. Peacock.

Garramone, Gina. 1985. "Effects of Negative Political Advertising: The Role of Sponsor and Rebuttal. *Journal of Broadcasting and Electronic Media* 29:147–159.

Garramone, Gina. 1986. "Candidate Image Formation: The Role of Information Processing." In *New Perspectives on Political Advertising*, ed. L. L. Kaid, D. Nimmo, and K. R. Sanders. Carbondale: Southern Illinois University Press.

Garramone, Gina M., Michael E. Steele, and Bruce Pinkleton. 1991. "The Role of Cognitive Schemata in Determining Candidate Characteristic Effects." In *Television and Political Advertising*, ed. Frank Biocca. Vol. 1, *Psychological Processes*. Hillsdale, N. J.: Lawrence Erlbaum Associates.

Geiger, Seth F. and Byron Reeves. 1991. "The Effects of Visual Structure and Content Emphasis on the Evaluation and Memory for Political Candidates." In *Television and Political Advertising*, ed. Frank Biocca. Vol. 1, *Psychological Processes*. Hillsdale, N. J.: Lawrence Erlbaum Associates.

Gilligan, Carol. 1982. *In a Different Voice: Psychological Theory and Women's Development.* Cambridge: Harvard University Press.

Goldenberg, Edie N. and Michael W. Traugott. 1984. *Campaigning for Congress.* Washington, D.C.: Congressional Quarterly Press.

Goldenberg, Edie N. and Michael W. Traugott. 1987. "Mass Media Effects in Recognizing and Rating Candidates in U.S. Senate Elections." In *Campaigns in the News: Mass Media and Congressional Elections*, ed. Jan Vermeer. New York: Greenwood

Goldenberg, Edie N., Michael W. Traugott, and Kim F. Kahn. 1988. "Voter Assessments of Presidential and Senatorial Candidates." Paper presented at the Midwest Political Science Association Meeting, Chicago, Ill.

Graber, Doris. 1989. *Mass Media and American Politics.* Washington, D.C.: Congressional Quarterly Press.

Hamilton, David L. 1979. "A Cognitive Attributional Analysis of Stereotyping." *Advances in Experimental Social Psychology* 12:53–84.

Hedlund, Robert D., P. I. Freeman, Keith Hamm, and R. Stein. 1979. The Electability of Women Candidates: The Effects of Sex Role Stereotypes." *Journal of Politics* 41:513–524.

Higgins, E. T., W. S. Rholes, and C. R. Jones. 1977. "Category Accessibility and Impression Formation." *Journal of Experimental Social Psychology* 13:141–154.

Hinckley, Barbara R., C. R. Hofstetter, and John Kessel. 1974. "Information and the Vote: A Comparative Election Study." *American Politics Quarterly* 2:131–158.

Huddy, Leonie. 1994. "The Political Significance of Voters' Gender Stereotypes." *Research in Micropolitics* 4:169–193.

Huddy, Leonie and Nayda Terkildsen. 1993. "Gender Stereotypes and the Perception of Male and Female Candidates." *American Journal of Political Science* 37:119–147.

Iyengar, Shanto and Donald R. Kinder. 1987. *News That Matters.* Chicago: University of Chicago Press.

Iyengar, Shanto, Mark D. Peters, and Donald R Kinder. 1982. "Experimental Demonstrations of the 'Not So Minimal' Consequences of Television News Programs. *American Political Science Review* 76:848 858.

Jacobson, Gary C. 1987. *The Politics of Congressional Elections.* Boston: Little, Brown.

Jacobson, Gary C. 1992. *The Politics of Congressional Elections* New York: HarperCollins.

Jacobson, Gary C. and Raymond Wolfinger. 1989. "Information and Voting in California Senate Elections." *Legislative Studies Quarterly* 14:509–524.

Johnson-Cartee, Karen S. and Gary Copeland. 1989. "Southern Voters' Reaction to Negative Political Ads in 1986 Election." *Journalism Quarterly* 66:188–193, 196.

Joslyn, Richard. 1984. *Mass Media and Elections.* Boston: Addison-Wesley.

Kahn, Kim Fridkin. 1991. "Senate Elections in the News: Examining Campaign Coverage." *Legislative Studies Quarterly* 16:349–374.

Kahn, Kim Fridkin. 1993. "The News Medium's Message: A Comparison of Press Coverage in Gubernatorial and Senate Campaigns." *Legislative Studies Quarterly* 20:23–36.

Kahn, Kim Fridkin and John Geer. 1994. "Creating Impressions: An Experimental Investigation of the Effectiveness of Television Advertising." *Political Behavior* 16:93–115.

Kaid, Lynda L. and Dorothy K. Davidson. 1986. "Elements of Videostyle: Candidate Presentations Through Television Advertising." In *New Perspectives on Political Advertising*, ed. L. L. Kaid, D. Nimmo, and K. R. Sanders. Carbondale: Southern Illinois University Press.

Kaid, Lynda L. and Keith R. Sanders. 1978. "Political Television Commercials: An Experimental Study of Type and Length." *Communication Research* 5: 57–70

Kathlene, Lyn, Susan E. Clarke, and Barbara A. Fox. 1991. "Ways Women Politicians Are Making A Difference." In *Gender and Policy-Making: Studies of Women in Office*, ed. Debra L. Dodson. Rutgers, N.J.: Center for the American Woman and Politics. Eagleton Institute of Politics, Rutgers University.

Kern, Montague. 1989. *30-Second Politics: Political Advertising in the 80s*. New York: Praeger.

Kinder, Donald R. 1983. "Presidential Traits." Pilot study report to the 1984 National Election Study (NES) manning committee and NES boards.

Kinder, Donald R. and David O. Sears. 1985. "Public Opinion and Political Action." In *Handbook of Social Psychology*, ed. Gardner Lindzey and Elliot Aronson. New York: Random House.

Kinder, Donald R., Mark D. Peters, Robert P. Abelson, and Susan T. Fiske. 1980. "Presidential Prototypes." *Political Behavior* 2:315–335.

Kinder, Donald R. and Thomas R. Palfrey. 1993. "On Behalf of an Experimental Political Science." In *Experimental Foundations of Political Science*. Ann Arbor: University of Michigan Press.

Klapper, Joseph. 1960. *The Effects of Mass Communications*. New York: Free Press.

Krosnick, Jon A. and Donald R. Kinder. 1990. "Altering the Foundations of Popular Support for the President Through Priming." *American Political Science Review* 84:497–512.

Lake, Cecilia. 1984. "Impact of Gender on Campaigns: A Study of Men and Women Candidates in 1982." Prepared for the National Women's Political Caucus, Washington, D.C.

Leeper, Mark S. 1991. "The Impact of Prejudice on Female Candidates: An Experimental Look at Voter Inference." *American Politics Quarterly* 19; 248–261.

Lippman, Walter. 1922. *Public Opinion*. New York: Free Press.

Locklsey, A., E. Borgida, N. Brekke, and C. Hepburn. 1980. "Sex Stereotypes and Social Judgment." *Journal of Personality and Social Psychology* 39:821–831.

Luntz, Frank I. 1988. *Candidates, Consultants, and Campaigns: The Style and Substance of American Electioneering*. Oxford: Basil Blackwell.

Markus, Gregory B. 1982. "Political Attitudes During an Election Year: A Report on the 1980 NES Study Panel Study." *American Political Science Review* 76: 538–560.

Markus, Gregory B. and Philip E. Converse. 1979. "A Dynamic Simultaneous Equation Model of Electoral Choice." *American Political Science Review* 73:1055–1070.

Markus, Hazel, M. Crane, S. Bernstein, and M. Saldi. 1982. "Self-Schemas and Gender." *Journal of Personality and Social Psychology* 42:38–50.

MacKuen, Michael. 1981. "Social Communication and the Mass Policy Agenda." In *More Than News*. Beverly Hills: Sage Publications.

MacKuen, Michael. 1983. "Political Drama, Economic Conditions, and the Dynamics of Presidential Popularity. *American Journal of Political Science* 26:165–192.

Martin, C. L. 1987. "A Schematic Processing Model of Sex Typing and Stereotyping in Children. *Child Development* 52:1118–1134.

McCombs, Maxwell E., and Donald Shaw. 1972. "The Agenda-Setting Function of Mass Media." *Public Opinion Quarterly* 36:176–187.

Mend, Michael R., Tony Bell, and Lawrence Bath. 1976. "Dynamics of Attitude Formation Regarding Women in Politics." *Experimental Study of Politics* 5:25–39.

Merrit, S. 1984. "Negative Political Advertising: Some Empirical Findings. *Journal of Advertising* 13:27–38.

Miller, Arthur, Martin Wattenberg, and Oksana Malanchuk. 1986. "Schematic Assessments of Presidential Candidates." *American Political Science Review* 79:359–372.

National Women's Political Caucus Survey. 1987. Washington, D.C.

Newhagen, John E, and Byron Reeves. 1991. "Emotion and Memory Responses for Negative Political Advertising: A Study of Television Commercials Used in the 1988 Presidential Election." In *Television and Political Advertising*, ed. Frank Biocca. Vol. 1, *Psychological Processes*. Hillsdale, N. J.: Lawrence Erlbaum Associates.

Okin, Susan Moller. 1990. "Thinking like a Woman." In *Theoretical Perspectives on Sexual Difference*, ed. Deborah L. Rhode. New Haven: Yale University Press.

Page, Benjamin I. and Calvin Jones. 1977. "Reciprocal Effects of Policy Preferences, Party Loyalties, and the Vote." *American Political Science Review* 73:1071–1089.

Page, Benjamin I., and Robert Y. Shapiro. 1987. "What Moves Public Opinion?" *American Political Science Review* 80:521–540.

Paletz, David L. and Richard J. Vinegar. 1977. "Presidents on Television: The Effects of Instant Analysis." *Public Opinion Quarterly* 41:488–497.

Patterson, Thomas E. 1980. *The Mass Media Election*. New York: Praeger.

Patterson, Thomas E. and Robert D. McClure. 1976. *The Unseeing Eye*. New York: Putnam.

Peterson, Trond. 1985. "Comment on Presenting Results from Probit and Logit Models." *American Sociological Review* 50:130–131.

Pfau, M. and M. Burgoon. 1988. "Inoculation in Political Campaign Communication." *Human Communication Research* 15:91–111.

Piereson, James E. 1977. "Sources of Candidate Success in Gubernatorial Elections: 1910–1970." *Journal of Politics* 39:939–958.

Poole, K. T. and L. H. Zeigler. 1985. *Women, Public Opinion, and Politics*. New York: Longman.

Popkin, Samuel L. 1991. *The Reasoning Voter: Communication and Persuasion in Presidential Campaigns*. Chicago: University of Chicago Press.

Pratto, Felicia and John Bargh. 1991. "Stereotyping Based on Apparently Individuating Information: Trait and Global Components of Sex Stereotypes Under Attention Overload." *Journal of Experimental Social Psychology* 27:26–47.

Rapoport, Ronald B., Kelly L. Metcalf, and Jon A. Hartman. 1989. "Candidate Traits and Voter Inferences: An Experimental Study." *Journal of Politics* 51:917–932.

Riggle, Ellen D., Victor C. Ottati, Robert S. Wyer, James Kuklinski, and Norbert Schwarz. 1992. "Bases of Political Judgments: The Role of Stereotypic and Nonstereotypic Information." *Political Behavior* 14:67–87.

Rinehart, Sue Tolleson. 1992. *Gender Consciousness and Politics*. New York: Routledge.

Robinson, Michael J. 1976. "Public Affairs Television and the Growth of Political Malaise: The Case of 'The Selling of the Pentagon.' " *American Political Science Review* 70:409–432.

Rosenwasser, Shirley Miller and Norma G. Dean. 1989. "Gender Role and Political Office." *Psychology of Women Quarterly* 13:77–85.

Rosenwasser, Shirley Miller, Robyn R. Rogers, Sheila Fling, Kayla Silvers-Pickens, and John Butemeyer. 1987. "Attitudes Toward Women and Men in Politics: Perceived Male and Female Candidate Competences and Participant Personality Characteristics." *Political Psychology* 8:191–200.

Schubert, Glendon. 1991. *Sexual Politics and Political Feminism*. Greenwich, Conn.: FAI Press.

Sapiro, Virginia. 1981–1982. "If U.S. Senator Baker Were a Woman: An Experimental Study of Candidate Images." *Political Psychology* 7:61–83.

Shapiro, Robert Y. and H. Mahajan. 1986. "Gender Differences in Policy Preferences: A Summary of Trends from the 1960s to the 1980s." *Public Opinion Quarterly* 50:42–61.

Sigal, Leon V. 1973. *Reporters and Officials: The Organization and Politics of Newsmaking*. Lexington, Mass.: D. C. Heath.

Sigelman, Lee and Carol K. Sigelman. 1984. "Sexism, Racism, and Ageism in Voting Behavior: An Experimental Analysis." *Social Psychology Quarterly* 45:263–269.

Sigelman, Lee and Susan Welch. 1984. "Race, Gender, and Opinion Toward Black and Female Presidential Candidates." *Public Opinion Quarterly* 48:462–475.

Smith, Eric R. A. N. and Peverill Squire. 1991. "Voter Sophistication and Evaluation of Senate Challengers." Presented at the American Political Science Association Annual Meeting, Washington D.C.

Spence, Janet T., Kay Deaux, and Robert L. Helmreich. 1985. "Sex Roles in Contemporary American Society." In *The Handbook of Social Psychology* 2:49–178, ed. Gardner Lindzey and Elliot Aronson. New York: Random House.

Spohn, Cassia and Diane Gillespie. 1987. "Adolescents' Willingness to Vote for a

Woman for President: The Effect of Gender and Race." *Women and Politics* 7:31–49.

Squire, Peverill. 1989. "Challengers in U.S. Senate Elections." *Legislative Studies Quarterly* 14:531–547.

Steeper, Fred T. 1978. "Public Response to Gerald Ford's Statements on Eastern Europe in the Second Debate." In *Presidential Debates: Media, Electoral, and Policy Perspectives*, ed. George F. Bishop, Robert Meadow, and Marilyn Jackson-Beeck. New York: Praeger.

Stein, Robert M. 1990. "Economic Voting for Governor and U.S. Senator: The Electoral Consequences of Federalism." *Journal of Politics* 52:29–53.

Stewart, Charles. 1989. "A Sequential Model of U.S. Senate Elections." *Legislative Studies Quarterly* 14:567–601.

Tajfel, H. 1969. "Cognitive Aspects of Prejudice." *Journal of Social Issues* 25:79–94.

Taylor, Shelley E. 1981. "A Categorization Approach to Stereotyping." In *Cognitive Processes in Stereotyping and Intergroup Behavior*, ed. David L. Hamilton. Hillsdale, N. J.: Lawrence Erlbaum Associates.

Taylor, Shelley E., Susan T. Fiske, Nancy L. Etcoff, and Audrey Ruderman. 1978. "Categorical and Contextual Bases of Person Memory and Stereotyping." *Journal of Personality and Social Psychology* 36:778–793.

Tidmarch, Charles M., Lori J. Hyman, and Jill Sorkin. 1984. "Press Issue Agendas in the 1982 Congressional and Gubernatorial Election Campaigns." *Journal of Politics* 46:1227–1242.

Thomas, Sue. 1991. "The Impact of Women on State Legislative Policies." *Journal of Politics* 53:958–976.

Trent, Judith S. and Robert V. Friedenberg. 1983. *Political Campaign Communication: Principles and Practices*. New York: Praeger.

Wadsworth, Anne Johnston, Philip Patterson, Lynda Lee Kaid, Ginger Cullers, Drew Malcomb, and Linda Lamirand. 1987. " 'Masculine' vs. 'Feminine' Strategies in Political Ads: Implications for Female Candidates." *Journal of Applied Communication Research* 15:77–94.

Weaver, David L., Doris Graber, Maxwell McCombs, and Eyal Chaim. 1981. *Media Agenda-Setting in a Presidential Election*. New York: Praeger.

Weber, D. H. and J. Crocker. 1983. "Cognitive Processes in the Revision of Stereotypic Beliefs." *Journal of Personality and Social Psychology* 36:778–793.

Welch, Susan, Margory M. Ambrosius, Janet Clark, and R. Darcy. 1985. "The Effect of Candidate Gender on Electoral Outcomes in State Legislative Races." *Western Political Quarterly* 38:464–475.

Wells, A. S. and Eleanor C. Smeal. 1974. "Women's Attitudes Toward Women in Politics: A Survey of Urban Registered Voters and Party Committeewomen." In *Women in Politics*, ed. Janet Jacquette. New York: John Wiley.

Westlye, Mark C. 1991. *Senate Elections and Campaign Intensity*. Baltimore: Johns Hopkins University Press.

Williams, John E. and Deborah L. Best. 1990. *Measuring Sex Stereotypes: A Multination Study*. Newbury Park: Sage Publications.

Witt, Linda, Karen M. Paget, and Glenna Matthews. 1994. *Running as a Woman: Gender and Power in American Politics*. New York: Free Press.

Wright, Gerald C., Jr. 1974. *Electoral Choice in America: Image Party and Incumbency in State and National Elections*. Chapel Hill: Institute for Research in Social Science, University of North Carolina.

Wright, Gerald C., Jr. and M. B. Berkman. 1986. "Candidates and Policy in U.S. Senate Elections." *American Political Science Review* 80:569–588.

Wyer, Robert S., Jr. and Thomas K. Srull. 1980. "The Processing of Social Stimulus Information: A Conceptual Integration." In *Person Memory: The Cognitive Basis of Social Perception*, ed. R. Hastie, T. Ostrom, E. Ebbesen, Wyer, D. Hamilton, and D. Carlston. Hillsdale, N. J.: Lawrence Erlbaum Associates.

Wyer, Robert S., Jr. and Thomas K. Srull. 1989. *Memory and Cognition in its Social Context*. Hillsdale, N. J.: Lawrence Erlbaum Associates.

Zanna, M. P. and S. J. Pack. 1975. "On the Self-Fulfilling Nature of Apparent Sex Differences in Behavior." *Journal of Experimental Social Psychology* 11:583.

Zipp, John F. and Eric Plutzer. 1985. "Gender Differences in Voting for Female Candidates: Evidence from the 1982 Election." *Public Opinion Quarterly* 49:179–197.

Index

advertisements. *See* political advertisements

agenda-setting: news coverage influencing, 12–13; by political advertisements for senate campaigns, 35. *See also* issues

aggressive ads. *See* attack advertisements

attack advertisements, gender differences in, 10; for gubernatorial campaigns, 33, 76–77, 145n3; for senate campaigns, 33–34, 38, 142n4

attire in political advertisements, gender differences in: for gubernatorial campaigns, 145n5; for senate campaigns, 32–33, 131

Baker, Howard, 9

behavior of candidates, stereotypes influencing, 2, 7, 11

Belaga, Julie, 90

bias, stereotypes encouraging, 4–5

Boschwitz, Rudy, 51, 120

Boxer, Barbara, 120, 129

Bradley, Tom, 90

Bryan, Richard H., 93

Cafferta, Patty, 93

campaign advertisements. *See* political advertisements

campaign context: electability of women candidates and, 2, 3, 117–30, 132; sex stereotypes and, 14–15, 30–42

campaign coverage. *See* news coverage

campaign resources, gender differences in news coverage and: for gubernatorial campaigns, 91–92, 97; for senate campaigns, 49, 91

campaign strategies: sex stereotypes influencing, 1, 10–11, 19–20, 131–33; for women candidates, 73–74, 134–37; for women senatorial candidates, 73–74

candidate status, voter's perception of candidates influenced by: gubernatorial candidates and, 112–14, 115; senate candidates and, 62–65, 67–69, 70–72

Carter, Jimmy, 12

Casey, Bob, 80

categorization, stereotypes confirming, 4–5

causal attribution, gender differences in, 7

challengers. *See* incumbents versus challengers

child welfare issues, gender differences:
  in gubernatorial campaigns, 78; in
  senate campaigns, 55
compassion in political advertisements,
  gender differences in: for
  gubernatorial campaigns, 81; for
  senate campaigns, 37, 38
competence in political advertisements,
  gender differences in: for
  gubernatorial campaigns, 78–79, 81,
  85, 96, 106; for senate campaigns, 37,
  38–39, 69

Deardourff, John, 81
defense issues. See national security
  issues
Deukmejian, George, 90

economic issues, gender differences in,
  35, 36, 37; in gubernatorial
  campaigns, 78, 79–80
education issues, gender differences in,
  35, 69; in gubernatorial campaigns,
  15, 78, 79, 80, 106, 107; in senate
  campaigns, 51, 55, 68, 69, 73, 106,
  145n10
experiments: on electoral consequences
  of campaign climate, 3, 117–30; of
  gender differences in news coverage
  of senate campaigns, 57–74; impact of
  stereotypes in campaigns assessed by,
  24–29; of potential advantage of
  women gubernatorial candidate,
  99–116; of sex stereotyping by voters,
  9–10
expressive strengths, of women, 6

failure, sex stereotypes related to, 7
feeling thermometer, voter attitudes
  toward women senate candidates
  assessed with, 119, 123, 125, 126,
  147n2
Feinstein, Diane, 33, 81, 129
"female" issues, 8–9, 10–11, 135–37;

attitudes toward women candidates
  and, 125, 126; in gubernatorial
  campaigns, 78–80, 83–85, 92–95,
  106, 107, 108; in senate campaigns,
  35–37, 40–41, 51–53, 55–56, 65, 67,
  68, 69, 106, 119–21, 123, 125, 126,
  128–30, 133, 135, 145n10
"female" traits, 9, 136; campaign
  strategies and, 10; in gubernatorial
  campaigns, 80–83, 95–97, 106–107,
  108, 111, 112, 113, 117; news
  coverage and, 14; in senate
  campaigns, 37–39, 41, 53–54, 55, 66,
  68, 69, 73–74, 107; sex stereotypes
  and, 6, 24
Fenwick, Millicent, 33, 76
foreign policy issues, gender differences
  in, 36, 37; in senate campaigns, 14,
  15, 51, 68

gaffes, news media's emphasis on, 12
Gantt, Harvey, 5
Goldschmidt, Neil, 88
government, quality of and women's
  election, 137–39
Grassley, Charles, 120
Growe, Joan, 120
gubernatorial campaigns, 3; electoral
  context and women candidates for,
  14–15; issues in, 14–15; news
  coverage and sex stereotypes
  influencing evaluation of, 25–29;
  news coverage of, 15, 22, 156–57;
  political advertisements for, 19–20,
  152. See also gubernatorial
  campaigns, gender differences in
  news coverage; gubernatorial
  campaigns, gender differences in
  political advertisements; issues,
  gender differences in
gubernatorial campaigns, gender
  differences in news coverage of, 14,
  83–85, 86, 87–98, 132–33: amount of
  coverage and, 13–14, 88–90, 97, 132;

Text: 10/13 Electra
Compositor: Columbia University Press
Printer: Braun-Brumfield
Binder: Braun-Brumfield